PAWS
& CLAWS

A Tale of Two Cats

PAWS
& CLAWS
A Tale of Two Cats

Audrey Duggan

BREWIN BOOKS

First published by
Brewin Books Ltd, 56 Alcester Road,
Studley, Warwickshire B80 7LG in 2013
www.brewinbooks.com

ISBN: 978-1-85858-507-9

A Cataloguing in Publication Record
for this title is available from the British Library

Typeset in Minion Pro
Printed in Great Britain by
4edge Ltd.

Contents

Foreword

As a dog lover there was a time, long ago, when I hardly considered cats at all. They were decorative and distant and little else – or so I thought. But that was then.

Later with the coming of Beau and Bunting, the former ethereal and white as fresh paint, the latter plump and the colour of gingerbread, perspectives shifted. For I was about to find out how wrong I had been and undergo a learning process which was to enrich my life.

It did not take long for me to become a proud cat convert, one that trumpeted the attributes of my two feline friends to anyone who would listen, even to those who would not. It did not take long for me to become a cat bore!

CHAPTER 1

Arrival

Beau came to us after we had spotted an advertisement in our local press.

"Good homes wanted for adorable cats and kittens."

At that time we had been without a cat for a number of months since the death of our beloved Jack or Jacket as he came to be called. He was a rescued three-legged black tom cat and it was through him that I started to enjoy the idea of cat ownership. The vacant knee, his bowl and bed were reminders of what we had lost but now perhaps was the time to move on – to remember the past but also to think of the future. So it was decided to pay those "adorable cats and kittens" a visit.

Upon arrival we were greeted by an amiable lady wearing wellingtons and an apron from top to toe. "Come in" she said "but be quick about it because I don't want the cats to run out" and she waved us on into what turned out to be the back room of a ground floor flat which looked out onto a small garden wired across from fence to fence like a cage.

The room was alive with cats. Cats at leisure on the settee, bunched together on the dining table and window gazing on the sill. Cats on top of cupboards, on and under chairs.

There were adults and kittens, long and short haired, black, tabby and marmalade – all looking for good homes.

It was as crowded in the tiny garden where cats grew in the borders; there climbed a stunted tree which reached its withered arms up through the netting; where a number had congregated on the miniscule terrace, waiting for the bell to ring – yes, she did ring a bell which summoned them to eat!

Our hostess brushed a wave of cats from the settee and invited us to sit down. We discovered that she never turned a cat away, that the oldest "inmate" was twenty-two! She explained that many were brought to her and that others were rescued by means of cat traps and the like. That at this moment there were sixty-two cats ballooning in her tiny home – but she hastened to add that ten of them were her own.

Filled with admiration we were fired up to make our choice. But where to start? Clearly we were going to need help. What sort of a cat did we have in

Beau.

mind? We were a little vague for like children in a toy shop we were spoilt for choice. What sex? What age? We did not mind. Did we have a dog? At last a positive response. We did have a dog, a very friendly dog and one that was used to cats. And then my eye was caught by a small white puff-ball with a tabby tip to its tail. Upon closer examination, the tail was complemented – no more than that – with a fleck of tabby on each ear.

He was not impressed by us. He puffed himself up a shade more and spat as we passed him by to "talk" to a young mackerel tabby with a torn ear. By now we had been with the "cat lady" for nearly an hour and were still undecided. A large Persian type female with a rumbling purr might be a good choice. Then, equally attractive, there was a sleek, black young tom – but that might remind us too much of what we had loved and lost. We returned to the puff ball. He watched our approach coldly…..

Our "cat lady" was becoming a little restless and in the end it was she who made our choice for us. "Bo Bo" she said, addressing the puff-ball "will be ideal for you" and she picked him up by the scruff of the neck prior to giving him a quick squirt from top to bottom, of flea repellent. Then, out of nowhere she "magicked" a cardboard box with a number of haphazardly punched holes, popped him inside and handed him over. "He doesn't seem very friendly," I said. "Oh he'll settle down. Give him a few days" she responded and waved us goodbye with what looked suspiciously like relief.

Bo Bo! He wouldn't keep that name for long I promised myself as I clutched the cat basket on my knee as we drove home. And so it was that he became Beau because he grew to be so beautiful. Beautiful enough for strangers to stop and admire him as he sunned himself on our front lawn. For motorists, when he chose to take his siesta in the lane (not encouraged), to slow down and circumnavigate the sleeping feline beauty, for to sound the horn would have been a kind of sacrilege. But this is to fast forward and I must begin at the beginning. A beginning that was to prove at best, problematic and at worst a near disaster.

CHAPTER 2

Early Days

Those early days and weeks were difficult as Beau's indifference to us was matched only by his antagonism towards Button, our dog. He would lie in wait for her behind half open doors or lurk in corners to pounce on her as our unsuspecting labrador sauntered by.

At first we put this down to his previously broken life. He had been found wandering the back streets of Birmingham during an especially cold winter. He had survived by drinking rain water from the gutter and pilfering a nearby rubbish dump for food. A cat trap had been set and it had taken many days before he was tempted, caught and taken into loving care.

And things were to get worse. Button, so named because of her bright-as-a-button eye and sunny disposition, was prepared to be friendly. Used to cats, there had always been one in the household since she joined our family, she expected to continue in her own delightful, unfussy and laid back way. But she was not allowed to. When she attempted to settle in her usual place on the hearth rug, Beau would be there before her – would rear up and spit. Then he took a liking to her food and would do his best, worst might be a more appropriate description, to prevent her access to her bowl. We grew tired of lifting a spitting, struggling cat by the scruff of his neck and re-positioning him in order that the charade might begin all over again. A month passed and we made little progress. Button grew stressed and fearful; took to spending more time alone in her basket in the kitchen. Now it began to seem as if the price we were paying for the privilege of owning our back street "moggie" was rising by the day and would soon become too expensive.

Meanwhile as we debated, Beau was thriving. He had put on weight and his coat had developed a lustre. He still did not think much of us, but accepted as his right, the proffered food and shelter. He was content, or seemed to be: the only member of the household who was.

By the time six weeks had gone by I had had enough. Beau was now attempting (unsuccessfully when we were around) to prevent Button from entering the living room at all and puffed up and spitting, was behaving like a jack-booted, feline little Hitler! It was time for action, so in a spurt of frustrated anger I fetched from the garage the cat basket that we had used to bring him home. I fetched it and placed it in pole position upon the kitchen table. Beau was to be returned. After lunch he would go. Let someone else cope with his tantrums.

We ate our lunch mournfully. Never defeated before, perhaps our expectations had been too high? Perhaps we had become smug because of the joy all our other pets had brought. Discussing our problem we munched on with Beau, as always, neatly tucked behind the breakfast room door, watching...... and listening.

Zero hour arrived, the cat basket with open door was primed and I moved to pick him up. But he had gone! No sign indoors or out. We hunted; checked and re-checked in all his favourite places: upstairs and down, indoors and out, under the beds and behind the settee, and even down at the bottom of the garden behind the shed where the dandelions flourished and tickled his nose as he fell asleep. Then with the realisation that he was not to be found, came relief. Harmony would be restored. The dog would no longer be anxious and life would return to normal. But this was to be followed by guilt. What had gone wrong? Where had we failed? Like the parents of a problem child we searched for answers.

At first I pretended that I did not mind what happened to Beau, but I did. For although he had been difficult, I had felt that trapped inside, but undeniably there, was a different animal if only the key to release it could have been found.

The hours passed and I returned the cat basket to the garage. Supper came and went; Button lay contentedly on the rug, her rug. Another day, another night and still no clue as to where he had gone, only a niggling unease to remind us that he had ever been part of the household. Then came the first hint that we had not seen the end of our back street prodigal after all. It was some days later and we were sitting after supper, relaxing. That was when we heard it – or thought we did.

From somewhere in the garden came a sound, a pathetic meow – and there it was again, low and tremulous. Soft and hesitant, it came again. Could it be? I ran to the window. Yes, it was. Beau was back! But what a different cat! No longer was he puffed up and preening, but abject. His coat was bedraggled, his brush of a tail "ratty" and his magnificent whiskers drooped. His egg shell blue eyes, once bright and blazing, were dulled and as he was let in, flicked a frightened glance in the direction of the kitchen table. No cat basket.

I picked him up, dried and then fed him his favourite white fish which he gulped down as if he had never eaten before. Then we watched, as very low to the ground, he crept into the living room and timidly approached the dog, licked her ear – a gesture graciously accepted – and settled down furthest from the fire.

Could it be that peace had broken out? We would soon find out and as it happened – it had. For it was from then that we were to begin to learn what an incredible, what a remarkable, what an affectionate and lovable animal Beau was to turn out to be. Inadvertently we had found the key and set him free. That is how it was.

CHAPTER 3

All in a Cat's Day

Beau's acceptance of our dog made life much easier. No longer did he bully and ambush but was content to take his place in the order of things. As the days passed, he came to realise that she was not a rival to be outclassed and outwitted but a companion, on occasion, even a champion as when she 'reminded' us that it was time for supper; his as well as hers. She forgave in the flick of an eye – was prepared to enjoy the present as if there had been no past and in the process taught us all a lesson in how to forgive and forget. No longer was she hesitant and withdrawn, but comfortable in her own space as the two settled down into a routine of agreeable harmony.

Then came Beau's acceptance of us. No longer were we tolerated as an unfortunate necessity: faceless providers of food and shelter. He developed a rumbling and deep throated purr. He watched us with interest, twined himself round legs and feet and jumped up on knees when any opportunity offered. This change of heart was soon reflected in his physical appearance. His whiskers regained their twanging elasticity and his white coat, fluffed like a giant powder puff, took on a magnetic sheen that blew with the wind and danced in the sun as he busied himself doing all the important things that a self respecting cat does!

Set into our terrace was, and is, a small goldfish pond and it was here, hidden among rockery plants that Beau would spend many happy hours. He soon became an expert fisherman – would wait, his chin balanced at the water's edge as over a saucer of milk. Here, searching for a telltale flash of colour or movement, his eye 'skewered' the depth. A paw dangled dreamily until in a sudden onslaught of tooth and claw another hapless victim was jerked from safety, and the unfortunate fish, dangling from his mouth like a couple of moustaches would be paraded up and down until the moment lost its appeal.

We would try to catch him. We chased, called, proffered an alternative menu in supplication. It was to no avail. He watched us with laughter in his eye and spurted away. Not to be outdone, we determined to stop this "game" and bought protective netting. This was then anchored under rockery stones and stretched across the pond.

The fish were safe – for two days! Then Beau bit a hole – a neat, round hole near the pool's edge. Again he lay in wait, managing on this occasion to "bag" Jaws the biggest and most prized of our remaining six fish; six that survived out of an original fourteen. Fortunately for Jaws, however, our cat with his "prize" then took refuge under our car parked on the drive and we were able to organise an ambush. With the aid of neighbours the vehicle was surrounded and Beau was hauled out with Jaws still clamped tightly in his mouth. The extricated fish was then re-cycled back into its pool where it is still swimming happily to this day.

Clearly, further action was needed. Something else must be done. So this time, a specially constructed, made-to-measure grid to fit the pond like a saucepan lid was ordered. It protected the fish which was good; but it looked as hideous as it was expensive which was bad. Now, sitting round the pool felt more like sitting beside a drain and although Beau's fishing expeditions had been brought to an abrupt stop, the item was soon dispensed with, leaving us back where we started. So it was back again to netting but this time tougher, stronger and plastic. It took Beau a trifle longer to cope with this, but it was only a matter of time. One day he managed to remove an inch or so of the material from its anchor and under the resultant flap was again able to dangle that "dreamy" paw.

And so things would have continued until all our fish had gone the same way to an untimely end, had it not been for the coming of Spring and the tit box in our neighbours' garden which was to provide an alternative attraction. Suddenly fishing was boring. Creatures that fly were to take over from those that swim. To sum up: "birding" was now "in" and fishing definitely "out".

Erected by David and Valerie, our friends and at that time neighbours, the tit box was placed near the opposite side of our hedge and as the parent birds flew back and forth with food for their hungry offspring, Beau decided to investigate. Up he scrambled and straddling the divide was to find himself in a prime position, not only to view the goings on outside but to interfere with the ongoing activity inside as well. He poked a tentative paw through the opening, fished around a bit and soon managed to extricate the first (and last) little victim which fell with a gentle plop to the ground.

Our neighbours rushed out. They were both enthusiastic members of Beau's ever increasing fan club but even so, his evil designs had to be thwarted. Our cat would outface a dog, a stoat or a fox when he felt like it, but one implement that did intimidate him was an upended garden broom.

So a 'broom patrol' was organised which proved mightily successful if rather onerous! It worked like this. As soon as Beau appeared on the top of the hedge, which at first was frequently, we took it in turns to rush down and wave the broom up his rear. Fortunately for us because it was both time consuming and hard work, the chicks grew quickly and in due course, six little blue tits were able to fledge and we were jubilant.

Beau was 'miffed' – until he discovered frogs. He became fascinated by the creatures as they made their way to spawn in our pond. He stationed himself along their route and patted them to see how far and how high they could be encouraged to jump. It was all too good to be true. Here he had his own real life 'jumping jack' toys! But the fun was short lived. The spawning season was brief and in any case, the wily creatures soon got wise to his little game and refused to budge. He tapped and tapped, poked and prodded, but all in vain, move they would not. Beau had met his match and conceded defeat with a flick of his tail as off he set on the lookout for entertainment of a more permanent kind.

So was our white cat kept busy and so long as things went his way – content.

CHAPTER 4

Lost and Found

Beau was fascinated by garden sheds; with what might be hidden underneath as well as the Aladdin's cave of goodies that he might discover within.

Underneath our shed lived a family of field mice whose activities provided him with an unfailing interest. They were safe enough so long as they remained 'at home' because Beau, try as he might, could not reach them; but when his pink nose was pressed close to the aperture between the wooden base of the shed and the ground, he could scent them and see them. Fortunately they soon got used to him, ignoring his gimlet eye and living their lives as if the said nose was of little consequence. And they knew better than to venture out until after dark when he was summoned in. But for a period and until his attention was caught by something else, there he was, ever hopeful, crouched and confident that one day there would come a time when they would lower their guard – which fortunately they never did.

The inside of our shed was even more intriguing, and when the door was open our pet never missed an opportunity to scurry inside as if he had some very important business to see to. Well, from his point of view, perhaps he did. For here he would explore dark crevices and corners, tickle his nose on cobwebs festooning them like decayed and long forgotten Christmas decorations. Here, too, the sweet scented trace of grass cuttings lingered and scurrying armies of spiders and beetles were his to prod and poke and pounce upon.

Beau would scrabble behind the garden spade and fork, scramble along dusty shelves or cradle himself in the empty box of the lawn mower. Our dark and dusty shed was his delight. Always on the verge of being tidied or cleaned out, it never was, which suited him just fine and was how it came to be his special place where, oblivious of time, he could live his 'real' and secret life; but always in tandem with that other one which offered him food and chin tickling and warmth in winter when the rains came and the snow.

So life continued along its untroubled way until one evening in summer when the grass had been mown and the mower returned to its rightful place, Beau did not respond to his nightly summons and his fish dinner remained uneaten. He was not to be found in any of his favourite places; behind the rockery from where he could spy upon any unsuspecting 'trespasser' cat who approached at its peril; or beneath the car from where he could safely challenge the oncoming headlights of approaching cars and see them off as they disappeared around the corner. He was nowhere to be seen.

We called and called and as minutes melted into hours, images of Beau as a pair of white fur gloves became a fixation. We tramped the streets calling his name; knocked on doors and besought our neighbours to check inside their sheds. The news spread that Beau had disappeared and up and down the road people walked down gardens, keys were turned and garden sheds flung open, all to no avail. Eventually we gave up and went to bed but not to sleep; and at three o'clock the next morning, I walked wearily for the last time round the garden. Nothing! So back to bed to toss and turn and with dread, to await the following day.

At first light I got up to let the dog out. Delighted with her early call, Button gambolled down the lawn, barking her greeting to the new day. Then she ran round the shed twice, wagging and sniffing as suddenly, as if from nowhere, there appeared in the window, a white cat! In the window of our own shed that we had checked so carefully the night before.

Beau in search of a little attention...

Unperturbed, Beau greeted us jovially, flourishing his tail and trotting briskly into the kitchen where he gobbled up an enormous breakfast. In spite of the dirt and the dust he was as clean and pristine as a freshly ironed sheet, perky as a Christmas card robin. Clearly he had enjoyed his night out and now he was returned to us with his ready purr at full throttle and his tail as fluffed as a feather duster, prepared to take up the cudgels of every day existence as if nothing had happened. For unlike his owners he did not have to face a day at work after a sleepless night. No, Beau did not have to work at all. But on second thoughts perhaps he did. There would be stranger cats to be warned off his territory – and a family of field mice to be guarded. He would have to visit the goldfish and there would always be birds, big, black birds to chase...... always something; for a cat's life, when not viewed from the human perspective is not so simple after all.

CHAPTER 5

Friends and Enemies

Most of Beau's friends were of the human kind – his enemies, feline. Most because as will be seen later, there were exceptions. One of his great friends was Roland, our vet, with the veterinary nurses at the clinic coming a close second. The reason, no doubt, was that he liked being the centre of attention and as a patient he was certainly that.

The adventure would begin in the waiting room where, sitting bolt upright in his cat basket, he would eye and take the measure of his rivals in theirs. Contemptuous of those who were curled up and behaving well, he would quickly transfer his attention elsewhere. His sweeping gaze would take in hamsters and rabbits, pet rats and dogs and when he saw a patient of sufficient merit, one that he might bait, he would stand up – puff up and rattle the door of his cat basket like a feline King Kong. Then it would not be long before I would be obliged to put an end to this nonsense by covering his basket with a blanket as if he were a pet canary.

It was not behaviour to be proud of and it was with relief that we finally would make it into the surgery where he became a different animal. For when he was lifted onto the table Beau developed a silky purr, his eye softened and his paws became velvet. It was then that the stroking and fussing diverted him from the plunge of the needle and it was with obvious regret, punctuated by a loud meow of protest, that he was forced to embark upon his homeward journey.

Beau's other friends of the human variety included many of the children and most of the adults who strolled past our front garden. There was Sam, our milkman, whose daily visits our cat anticipated to the second, jumping down from our wall and lightly up on to his float. Cows' milk is not an ideal food for cats and too much can be harmful. But Beau did not know this and neither did Sam who every week would lower a brimming saucer, brought specially for the occasion, and not budge until the last drop had disappeared down the animal's throat. A treat that caused no apparent harm and a great deal of pleasure to them both.

Now if Beau's human friends were many so, sadly, were his enemies among the cat population. For although neutered Beau, like most males, was very territorial and early in the day could be seen marking out his territory, targeting every bush, brier and plant with a well directed squirt and a wriggle. In this way "no admittance" was signposted around our garden and woe betide any unknown cat who strayed across the border. Should this happen a choreographed series of happenings was triggered. Both animals would freeze and then, arching sideways, proceed slowly and crabwise towards each other and the inevitable confrontation. This would take the form of a tight, white ball of fury as Beau, emitting a screech like a demon from Hell, all teeth and claws, would launch himself at the unwelcome visitor. So did our pet successfully manage his affairs, protect his borders and keep for himself the sunlit quiet of his suburban garden.

All went as planned until the day that Boss Cat arrived! Until one bright summer's morning, he suddenly appeared on top of our garden shed. Boss Cat was an unneutered male. An enormous tabby with whiskers from ear to ear which he wore with the rakish air of a buccaneer. His coat was sleek and well oiled. His muscles rippled and his movements were lithe. It was soon clear that he had little time for humans and even less time for other cats which he would despatch with a flick of his claw. Unless he had designs......
and designs he had on Beau!

From his vantage point on top of the shed he watched and waited – and dominated. Beau's ball of fury cut no ice with him. Beau's demon shriek he dismissed as a mere aberration. It was a sad fact but true, that no longer was our pet the master of all he surveyed. That was bad enough, but worse was to follow: for finally, as Boss Cat jumped down and sauntered towards him up the garden, he was frightened. Ours was a small cat and his puff ball act had been exposed as a sham; his dramatics dismissed with a casual flick of an alien tail. Overnight our garden was not "his" garden any longer and we watched Beau physically shrink as his confidence diminished.

After a confrontation which he lost decisively, our pet retreated indoors. Day after day he ventured no further than the kitchen door. He drooped. Again his coat lost its lustre. Meanwhile Boss Cat reigned. He reclined by the pond where Beau had fished. He climbed Beau's apple tree, exulted in the sun on Beau's dappled lawn. He was to be found sleeping among the nasturtiums, behind the foxgloves or hunting in the shrubbery; all favourite haunts of our little white cat.

Days passed and his situation hopeless, Beau visibly dwindled. He would not eat and spent his time, watching his rival from behind curtained windows. Something had to be done – but what? Where did Boss Cat come from? If we could find his owner that would be a start. We asked around among neighbours and friends who were eager to commiserate but could offer little practical help. They agreed that Beau's loss of self esteem was making him ill – one only had to look at the animal to see that – but could offer little practical help.

Then someone suggested a cat trap, but as Boss Cat was sleek and well fed the idea was rejected. We took further advice. We even contacted the local rat catcher but changed our minds because we did not want the animal harmed. Meanwhile we returned home every day to our little bundle of misery – dirty white, with his pink nose pressed to the window like a leech.

Then came a breakthrough. Somebody vaguely remembered seeing a large, sleek, tabby cat sunning himself in a shop window. Where? Which shop? They could not remember. Even so we were encouraged to inquire locally and then widen the search to take in premises within a three mile radius. Always we drew a blank. Until one day, the seemingly impossible happened. That morning I opened the curtains and the roof of the garden shed was vacant! No Boss Cat. For weeks we had played unwilling hosts to a swaggering feline cavalier and now he was not there. Down we went and searched everywhere. Behind, beside and inside the shed, the potting compost and another of Beau's haunts, the greenhouse. Of Boss Cat there was no sign. We were baffled.

Days later a possible explanation emerged. We learned that a local funeral director had sold up and left, that he had kept his cat on the premises – a large tabby as a rat catcher. Was this the answer? It was certainly true that we never saw Boss Cat again and that all the facts fitted. But we were cautious.

And if we had problems, so did Beau. Like a man with a broken leg he had to learn again how to "walk". He had to reclaim his own. It took time. He would creep outside and rush back in; but gradually periods in the garden lengthened until the time came when he began again to mark his territory. Then we knew that we were heading for the finishing line! And it was not to be long before Beau's coat regained its snowy lustre and the banner of his tail was again held high.

Soon he rediscovered his puff ball act and his "demon screech" returned. The nightmare was over. Indoors the chin tickling, the piano playing (he had developed a liking for running up and down the keys) and television viewing (he enjoyed watching the movement) were resumed. The rumble of his purr returned.

Our pet had come back to us. Hurray!

CHAPTER 6

Interlude

By now we had had the pleasure of Beau's company for nearly two years. He had matured into an extremely handsome fellow with a long haired fluffy coat and a tail like an upheld banner as he raced towards us, which he did frequently to show his affection by twining himself round ankles and head butting our shins to get attention. He was a great explorer and frequently to be seen in woods several miles away which could only be reached by crossing a busy main road. This was worrying, but for our pet there were advantages; as his territory increased so did his fan club. He grew used to being praised and petted, indeed expected it.

Beau thrived upon attention and adulation and would perch on the wall of our front garden, rearing his head to be stroked as people walked by. Should this be misunderstood he would meow loudly to indicate what was required and, on occasion, even allow children to pick him up so long as they put him down the instant he determined. Should they resist, a loud yowl and a gentle nip would indicate his displeasure.

On one occasion Beau was to be seen, sitting placidly in the arms of a small child – a toddler of around three years old. Gently, I asked her where she was going and her response that she was taking the "pretty pussy cat" home as a brother for her pet rabbit was sufficient for him to be carefully removed and "posted" indoors before he had time to demonstrate his displeasure. Soon Beau was to become known as the "roll over pussy" and the little boy who coined the phrase is now a high flying civil engineer in Saudi Arabia. This all began because our pet had now taken, not only to arching his neck, but to lying down and exposing his tummy to be tickled! Everybody complied.

In fact we all became so well trained, that when Beau decided to take his afternoon siesta in the middle of our road, no driver would toot. All slowed down and careful not to disturb him would mount the pavement instead! So it was that our cat, already pleased with himself, grew to believe that he was invincible.

It now became clear that Beau had taken a fancy to cars, or to be more precise, newly driven ones with warm bonnets. Cars that had just returned from shopping or work suited very well and often friends and neighbours would wait to garage their vehicles until our pet deigned to clamber down. Otherwise cat and car might be seen slowly sliding garagewards in the hope that the former might take the hint.

Only once was I really concerned. This was when cat and car were seen speeding down the road and there was nothing to be done but to give chase. Fortunately, it did not take long for the appalled driver to realise his mistake, screech to a halt, and the terrified cat to be transferred from his vehicle to ours. There was no question of the animal jumping down or running off. He was, quite literally, rigid with fear; legs like spikes and a tail like a broom handle. But one good thing to come out of it was that Beau realised his bonnet hopping days were over – forever.

There were compensations. Indoors Beau decided to concentrate upon his musical bent. He had earlier taken a liking to the piano and would run up and down the keys, revelling in the resultant cacophony. Fortunately it was a craze that soon ended and now he would sit quietly to one side and gently pat a note here and there to produce "tiptoe" sounds of delicacy and uncertainty. Then there was television. He was fascinated by the moving pictures on the

Beau in bloom!

screen and as a great fan, his viewing was far from selective. He enjoyed nature programmes, especially those concerned with big game; the bigger the better. Lions, tigers, polar bears; he watched them all from a crouched position on the settee as if prepared to pounce.

Another of his delights were visitors. When told who was coming he would station himself in the hall, fixing the front door with an insistent and intrepid stare. Friends had to be warned of what would happen, because as soon as they stepped inside, he would hurl himself at them in a rugby tackle, so keen was he to be picked up and petted.

Indoors he invented his own games. One of his favourites was to play with "his" cotton reels. He had quite a collection and with a straight paw would "bat" them, one at a time, from one end of the room to the other. It was a pastime that kept him happy when there was little else to occupy him; one which made us think that he thought in the same way as our dog because they spent so much time together.

In the winter the lively flames of a crackling fire would hold him in thrall. Showing no fear he would creep closer and closer, to drop down with his chin on cushioned paws, his eyes boring deeply into the burning recesses of beyond. Until sleep put an end to it, there he would lie, hot as a roasted chestnut, in spite of all efforts to persuade him to budge.

Another hobby was window gazing. Our pet would station himself on an upper window sill (more god-like) and from his vantage point watch and "swear" at every bird that flew, swooped or perched on a nearby branch. He watched mothers and prams, children trundling toys. But most of all he searched with his "I spy" eye for unwanted cats (they were all unwanted) so that he could map from where they came and where they might go for future reference.

But best of all, come summer, he liked to be out of doors, lazing in the sun, feigning sleep. In a world where insects whirred and zoomed among the foxgloves there he was, among all the action, seemingly indolent. But his one cocked ear and pink, quivering nose told a different story. For nothing happened on these long, sleepy and sunny days that did not register. From ladybirds to scurrying beetles; an army of ants to bees and wasps and worms; all were noted and all served to complete and enrich his day.

So the weeks and months passed as Beau blossomed into his prime. Like lightening they sped and now it was not to be long before another feline friend was to enter our household and become the third member of our animal family.

CHAPTER 7

Bunting

Beside the river, if a muddy stream that meandered its way across a nearby park might be dignified by that name, Button and I would often take our morning walk. Labradors are water dogs and ours was no exception. She enjoyed a paddle and when sticks were thrown would plunge delightedly into the water to retrieve them.

One morning we were returning home after a particularly satisfactory (from her point of view) session when we came across two little tow headed boys of around six and eight years old. As it was half term, there was nothing unusual in this, except that the elder was carrying, very carefully, a cardboard shoe box. The dog and I watched them as they headed for where the water formed a bowl in a bend of the stream, as walking purposely they targeted the spot where the river ran deep. What, I wondered, could be in the box being carried with such care towards the brink?

"What have you got there?" I asked with a smile. The child did not hesitate but opened the lid to reveal, plump and placid, a ginger kitten of around eight weeks old. Then, before I had time to pose the obvious question he lisped an answer "We are going to dwown it!" Soon the sorry little story was complete. Their father had despatched his children on this particular errand along with doing some shopping when the deed was done. "Drown the kitten and buy me a packet of cigarettes and some crisps" he had said – or something like that.

By now the children had arrived at the river's edge. "Is this deep enough?" asked the elder boy, his eyes wide. "I've got a better idea" I responded. "You give the box to me and tell your daddy that you gave the kitten away as a present to a lady". Without a word the precious cargo was handed over and the children, relieved of their burden, and now with nothing to think about but a packet of crisps ran light heartedly away. So it was that Button's morning walk turned into a rescue operation and the two of us became three for our journey home.

Because he was such a baby, we called our new little one, Bunting. Bunting who was destined to give us seventeen years of joy and happiness. But that is to race ahead and at this point it was clear that before we could face the future there would be problems to overcome. One of the most immediate of these was food; and another, no less pressing, was Beau, or to be more precise, the uncertainty of how he would react when he first saw the little stranger.

Would feeding present a difficulty? The kitten was so very young – too young to have left his mother and already before we arrived home, I was imagining nightly feeds from the stopper of a fountain pen (if such an old fashioned device could be found) and wondering how we would be able to cope. Fortunately such worries were to prove unfounded. Stockpiled in the kitchen were Beau's assorted tins of delight – or more accurately – tins that had once been a delight and were now rejected. He was a faddy eater.

I was doubtful, very doubtful, but we had to begin somewhere and so I decided to "try out" the new comer with a spoonful of Whiskers. This was duly mashed with a drip of milk into a saucer and placed out of reach of the dog. Then we waited as released from the prison of his box, the little one approached as rapidly as his podgy legs would allow. We watched as he sniffed, made a snuffling sound…… and "scoffed" the lot! A second and then a third spoonful was quickly proffered and despatched in the same way, until, finally, the tin was empty. He was going to be a mighty eater, this little one!

What a busy life I lead! Bunting takes a well earned rest.

So that was one problem solved, but what of the second, potentially much more serious? How would Beau react? What sort of welcome from that quarter would be forthcoming? When I returned home, Beau had been in his usual place playing mouse catcher at the bottom of the garden. But not for long, for when he heard the front door open he rushed to welcome us. He approached and sniffed the shoe box with mild interest – watched its occupant emerge with something approaching fascination. Then he sniffed the kitten a little, licked a little which quickly became a lot. Head, ears, back, abdomen and tail – the whole kitten came in for a thorough cleaning. Altogether a good thing we agreed, reminding the little one of its mother.

When we fed Bunting we had the presence of mind to feed Beau as well. It was a gesture much appreciated as it was nowhere near his meal time and he determined to make the most of it. It was also a signal that our white cat was not going to be marginalised.

So was Bunting accepted from the start; and possibly because he was so very tiny (he had yet to fill the palm of an adult hand), and posed no threat, he was always to be afforded shelter beneath the umbrella of Beau's protection. But there was a price to pay: there always is! The little one had to learn to fit in and understand that his role was to be a subordinate one.

Time passed and on the whole Beau developed into a kindly disciplinarian who taught by example. Bunting was shown the cat tray and how to stand by the door when he wanted to be let out. However, the elder cat was quick to nip or wrestle the kitten to the ground should he step out of line. Should he inch too near the fire or inadvertently occupy Beau's place on the settee.

And so it was that Bunting grew rapidly from a placid roly-poly kitten into an equally plump and mild tempered adult, during which time he was initiated into the activities of a respectable cat's life in suburbia. Padding around after Beau he was introduced to our brightly coloured fish as they stormed around their pool; to the under shed family of field mice with their pin bright eyes where, fortunately, hours of waiting to catch them went unrewarded.

But in spite of Beau's persistence, there were some skills that Bunting would or could not master. Our white cat was a great tree climber and top of the fence runner. Bunting would attempt neither. He was frightened of heights and suffered (apparently) from vertigo! He was content to sit and watch as Beau, with the dexterity of a sailor climbing the crow's nest, ran up and down apple trees in a flash or skittered along the pencil edges of the fence without a care. Throughout his life Bunting was to remain stolidly earthbound to find his pleasures where earthworms dug for victory and the fronds of grasses tickled his nose.

Our second cat was not adventurous – well hardly ever. He preferred to live his life in the slow lane and admire from afar the antics of our first. Even so, on occasion he was to surprise us as will become clear...... "Still waters run deep" we are told and sometimes, plump and placid marmalade cats have been known to fit into this category.

CHAPTER 8

Beau Time

"Normal" for Beau were the highs and lows – the ups and downs of his feline existence. The highs were very high and the lows equally low; the pendulum swings of his moods so exaggerated that, at times, we wondered if we had a schizophrenic cat. Upon reflection we did not, for things were simpler than that. Like many humans he was a delight when he got his own way and a terror when he did not! A fact which reminds me of the nursery rhyme about the little girl with the curl, who:

When she was nice she was very very nice
And when she was not she was horrid

Lines that sum up our beautiful Beau perfectly.

Take last Tuesday, for example. Beau had been in and out – out and in until I lost count, his behaviour consistent only in so far as he always wanted to be where he was not. He would appear at the door to be let out and at the window to be let in a few moments later. He wanted food. He did not want food and then in a seemingly endless merry-go-round of feline indecision, he wanted the garden – again! I had had enough! I was preparing a lecture and, at last, determined to ignore him.

This was to prove difficult. Our white cat pressed his face up against the patio window. His mouth opened in a large meow. Nothing happened so he changed tactics. A gentle head butting against the glass produced a low velocity thrumming which after a period of time became increasingly difficult to ignore. But I did. So he changed tactics again.

At first Beau had determined that I was deaf or stupid or both. So he did not become angry until it became clear that I was neither and he was, in fact, being ignored. This took time for he was so used to having his every wish anticipated and when, at last, this unpalatable truth dawned, he was furious. He fastened his attention upon the door handle and stared hard, considering its shape and distance from the ground. Then he flew at it – jumped up with outstretched paws to grab at it and missing it slowly slithered back down to land, scratching the glass as he did so. Again and again, up he jumped to slither downwards as the elusive handle persisted in slipping from his grasp (paws). Up, scratch and slither – so it went on until my nerve failed and in desperation I flung open that wretched patio door to let him come in, which he did, the black cloud of his mood in striking contrast to the brilliant white of his coat.

Beau was angry, but magnanimous in victory, he decided to forgive my waywardness - flicked up his tail, fixed me with an egg shell blue eye ablaze with triumph and demanded, via the kitchen window, to be let out! So was the morning wasted and my lecture unprepared. But the mini drama that had been played out did serve to reinforce what we already knew, that our white cat was a highly intelligent animal who worked things out. It served to make me curious about other things that he could or would learn to do.

That the door handle operated the opening of the door was one. That the curtains blocked light and vision was another and he frequently could be seen moving window nets with a paw to get a better view. He developed a large (for a cat) vocabulary and we worked out that there were at least seven words or phrases by which he recognised meal times. "Fish fish" would have him come running as would "biscuits", "dinner" and "time to eat". He also understood "bedtime", "come along", "go on" and "no". Then there were endearments and encouragement such as "good boy" and "well done" which would guarantee a positive response: a loud purr or his narrow eyed attempt at a smile. Cats haven't the facial muscles to smile as we do, but to indicate pleasure Beau would first open his eyes wide and then narrow them to the merest slits, gestures he would repeat should we respond with a smile. Then there were his different types of purr – each to suit different occasions. When sitting contentedly on a knee he would indulge us with a deep, breathy purr, one that with its rhythmic rise and fall induced a pleasing sense of relaxation, even sleepiness. In anticipation of a meal his purr would become light and jerky and as he was about to fall asleep he produced a gentle vibrating throb.

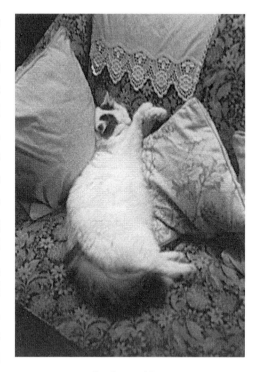

In the lap of luxury.

Once asleep, however, the register would constantly change dependent upon the dream that he was experiencing: increased volume and rapidity when "hunting", a smooth rumble when dreaming of sunlit meadows. Indeed so distinct was the different speed, volume and range of his responses that it was almost possible to plot what he was doing and where in his dreams he was going.

Another way in which our cat communicated could be explained by the fact that he was an excellent "guard dog" and would emit a "growl", a sound somewhere between a yowk and shriek when someone he did not know arrived at the front door. Then if, as was frequently the case, the "stranger" was invited in he would continue to make strange chuntering sounds until convinced that no harm was intended. But once convinced, in the blink of an eye he became again the "roll-over" pussy so beloved by children; milky eyed and bushy tailed, proffering his tummy in an invitation to be stroked.

How different was this from Bunting's world. Not for him were the dangers of distant woodlands, the constant threat to the ego, that pride of hierarchy that came with the necessity of being a top cat. His world was uncomplicated and in a way more pleasurable. Not for him were the rewards of victory and the ravages of defeat. He knew his place and, entirely without aspiration, was content with his place at the bottom of the pile. And how he had grown. Over the years he had developed into a magnificent ginger tom with wide chestnut eyes and whiskers like the moustaches of a cavalry officer – splendid but not at all in keeping with his personality as sunny as a warm summer's day. Bunting adored Beau and was content to live his life without the thrills, confined by choice to the reassuring presence of his flower pots.

So did both cats thrive. Bunting as follower and Beau as purposeful leader.

CHAPTER 9

Bunting and Beau

Although so different in temperament, the one light and mercurial, the other plump and placid, our two cats quickly became great companions. It was soon a familiar sight to see "the little one" padding around in the wake of his elder "brother".

It will be remembered that Beau's every day started punctually with the marking out of his territory, a routine that the new kitten quickly learned. Bunting would watch the older cat mark every bush and shrub with his usual wiggle and squirt; and long before he understood what it was all about was soon walking behind and imitating Beau's every move – a double act as amusing as it was unbelievable!

Bunting was less extrovert and more timid than our white cat. His nightly excursions seldom took him beyond the perimeter of the flower pots that graced the front of our bow window. But they both had clocks in their stomachs, and come supper time, would arrive indoors together; Beau from his exploration of woodlands far away (a mile at least) and Bunting from the safer confines of the front garden.

At six o'clock, there they were, drooling and ready; muscles tensed and tails quivering as they watched their dishes descent. And then the game began. First they would reject what was on offer. A few suspicious sniffs followed by a single desultory mouthful until after a few sneaky glances at the other's plate, the temptation of forbidden fruit became irresistible. This was because they enjoyed stealing and it was never long before the alternative saucer became a magnet. Each would sidle across and eat his fill- gobble up as quickly as possible because thieves have to be smart, and then settle down somewhere private to digest his "stolen" meal!

Owning pernickety pets is a situation with which most cat owners are familiar. In supermarkets they are to be seen huddled, with furrowed brow in front of an array of tinned and packaged products, most with beguiling pictures of pampered pets on the front – cats that look content, eat without demur all their kind owners give them.

But not in real life where pet owners pick up and put down indecisively. For all of us know that feeding cats is like playing golf: that Monday's success can, and frequently does, turn into Tuesday's failure. Dry food or wet? Packaged or tinned? Good for the teeth, dry food can be bad for the kidneys. Tinned food, on the other hand, is likely to contain colour and that is also bad. The permutations seem endless and many of us solve the problem by buying both and hoping for the best! As a treat, Bunting and Beau were fed on home cooked white fish, and whether they ate straight away, or whether they did not, our pets remained sleek and in Bunting's case also plump which was, one supposes, the purpose of spoiling them in this ridiculous fashion.

Food played an important part in the lives of our cats, but there was much else on offer to brighten up their day. Take birding for example; a pursuit that furnished Beau with hours of entertainment, but one for which Bunting showed little aptitude. He was too slow, too bumbling and held his tail too high, signalling his intent as the birds flew away.

One sunny morning Beau had been busy among a shower of starlings, scattering them to make a broken rainbow as their glinting wings rose and fell. Fortunately his efforts were unsuccessful but his actions were to set the scene for what was to follow.

Later that morning a single starling ventured purposefully across the lawn, catching Bunting's eye as with tail up he inched slowly closer. Meanwhile from up in the trees eyes were watching. Seconds passed and the cat positioned himself to pounce. Then it happened! Bunting launched himself; missed of course, and was "dive bombed" as from tree after tree a screeching rain of birds descended. With open beaks and wings flapping they encircled the terrified animal who, by now immobile with fear, sank into a miserable heap.

The attack lasted, at most, a couple of minutes when as if on cue and with mission accomplished, the birds flew up and away to a hearty chortle and chatter in their tree tops. Bunting remained inert. Was he hurt? Was he dead? Out I ran to bring indoors and to safety the little bundle of misery. By now he was shaking violently and his eyes remained shut as if to block out the misery of what had happened.

We kept him warm and after some time persuaded him to sip a little milk, even toy with a morsel of food. And of course he recovered; but it took a couple of days before he could be encouraged to leave the house. The starlings had had their revenge but on the wrong cat! From Bunting they had little to fear but as birds do not distinguish between one cat and another, Beau, the guilty one who had frightened the birds earlier, sat safely indoors, eyes wide with excitement while poor, harmless Bunting took the punishment. Such is life.

More sedentary occupations were also popular, especially the yoga sessions. Both cats would join me as I meditated. First would come Beau to perch on one knee to be swiftly followed by Bunting who wrapped himself around the other and we all three contemplated together – the cats, no doubt, thinking about food, until the clock spoke and it was time to go, time for the throbbing purrs to stop.

In the summer it was frequently siesta time and each cat had his favourite space. Bunting would curl up where the long grass tickled his nose, playing tiger among the weeds around the compost heap. Beau, on the other hand, was more aesthetically inclined. For him there was always a quiet nook

Keeping order!

among the roses where buzzing bees and zinging insects lulled him to sleep. There they would settle for hour upon hour, without regret and innocent of the human admonishment not to waste time.

As light relief, it was Beau who introduced Bunting to the delights of butterflies and bumble bees. Light and balletic, he would dance after then on his hind legs, or crouch and pounce from behind the foxgloves where deep inside their enticing trumpets insects were busy. Slower and heavier, Bunting was poor at butterflies and, I am glad to say, even worse at bumble bees. But he entered into the spirit of the game and although he was never able to jump sufficiently high and always pounced too late, no doubt he deserved a mark for trying.

By now both cats were known up and down the road. Beau, the "roll over" pussy and Bunting the "teddy bear" who, unlike our white cat, did not sit sentinel on our front garden wall, did not when a likely child came along, roll over and wave his paws in the air, waiting for a stroke and a tickle. Instead, the more timid Bunting waited and watched from behind his flower pots, emerging when he deemed it safe for a pleasant word or two from an elderly lady or gentleman before retreating again into the shadows.

Beau was more sociable but even he had to be in the right mood. One day a neighbour of ours, an elderly gentleman who was a great cat lover, made the mistake of stroking our pet when he was stretched out on our front wall in a deep sleep. From a world of giant butterflies and limitless green ways, of shafting sunlight and the scent of roses, he awoke with a start to deliver a bayonet slash across the base of the old gentleman's thumb. Then, rigid with disapproval he rose up and stalked away to disappear and resettle himself where undisturbed he might continue his fragmented dreams. All this was recounted to us by Mr Everson, "the victim", who wore a large plaster and even larger smile to reassure us that there was no ill will. "I should have left him alone, I frightened him" he said as he sat in our living room with a mug of coffee, where Beau, now in a friendly mode rolled on the settee, his silk soft paws and eyes as mild as milk, belying his earlier "aberrant" behaviour and signalling that all was forgotten. We apologised of course, and all agreed that our cat had behaved "out of character".

Out of character or not, there was no doubt that Beau did have a darker side. While Bunting would take flight rather than engage, the former's moods were more in evidence. He determined to be fed first, stroked first and, if wet, dried before either the dog or the other cat. His concerns were personal: Bunting's were different and involved those things which he would rely upon us to sort out. He would get wedged behind the settee, or shut in the wardrobe. He would have to be extricated from behind the back of the lawn mower in the garden shed. He was the least nimble of cats but one of the most lovable.

But on the whole, both animals were happy – and why should they not be? They lived in a world geared to their needs and if they were spoiled, it is arguable that they deserved it for the pleasure that they gave which outweighed all else. "All else" that will emerge later on.

CHAPTER 10

The Wobbly Tree

A friend and her dog were invited round – the latter a well meaning animal but a bit "bouncy" because he was young. We were sitting in the garden and Boswell, of the terrier type, was champing contentedly on a chewy. Button was snoozing and Beau, leopard like on a low branch managed to be part of and, at the same time not part of, the little group until he chose to disappear quietly into the garden shed.

It was a sunny afternoon with, from our point of view, nothing much happening but a great deal if you were a cat in a dusty shed. For the scurrying beetle, the woodlouse and earwig, not always especially attractive to us, provided Beau with a constant challenge as he nosed around in the dust veiled dark of that other world. A crowded arena of constant insect activity and one of which he would be king.

So much for Beau, but what of Bunting? We assumed that he was lulled asleep, contentedly out of sight in the long grass. For a while he may have been until suddenly he chose to trundle out with tail up and paw outstretched after a quarry of his own – a butterfly! He missed of course – but that was not the point. The effect on Boswell was what mattered. For him it was a gesture too far as revving into top gear he, too, gave chase. Harmless it was – fun it may have been but from Bunting's perspective things looked very different.

Terrified and desperate to make his escape, and with much slipping and sliding, he managed to scrabble some way up our fir tree. Too far up for one of us to reach him and, as it turned out, too far up for his own peace of mind as limpet like he stuck fast, hanging on and hardly able to breathe. Pumped with adrenaline and mindless of all else, his scramble up had found him for the first and only time in his life up a tree, in a "dizzying" situation from which he was too frightened to extricate himself even when the danger was over.

Boswell was removed indoors and we remained to plead with our cat to return to earth. But it was no use. At first we were not unduly concerned, the animal would come down in his own time and we continued with our tea. But as time wore on and the minutes turned to hours and the hours lengthened and there he remained, we began to see things differently. One thing became clear. Stuck fast or nearly stuck fast, for occasionally he would slither a little, scrabble and wobble, Bunting was not going to budge – he was not going to come down.

At last, the final sandwich eaten, our guilt ridden friend was obliged to leave and we were left alone with our problem. From the ground we held up bowls of his favourite food. Tuna? Liver? Saucers of milk? He did not budge. We even encouraged Beau who was delighted to oblige, to scamper up the wretched tree and down again to prove how easy (for a cat) the exercise was! A waste of time.

Bunting clung on. By now it was dark and we were taking it in turns to be on duty under the tree; encouraging, cajoling and beseeching our pet to change his mind. We could no longer see him, but his piteous cries could be heard by half the neighbourhood and a group of well wishers had gathered round the base of his "prison" as if at a wake. Boswell's owner returned and together our craned necks grew painful. A ladder was fetched and propped against the trunk, but it did not reach sufficiently high and our cat wobbled precariously as his would-be-rescuer peered into the gloom, teetered on the top rung with outstretched arms.

Then someone remembered an advertisement featuring a kind fireman rescuing a kitten trapped in a drain. So we rang the Fire Brigade. The response was not encouraging; and it soon became clear that their brief did not include rescuing a ginger tom cat from a fir tree at the bottom of our garden. Kittens and drains, yes; Bunting from his prison in a tree, no. Meanwhile down on earth, cups of tea were distributed to keep up our spirits. By this time Bunting's cries had reached a crescendo but he still stuck fast, his eyes like lamps in the flickering torchlight directed to find out where he was.

Then another idea surfaced. Could the animal be frightened down? Somebody's son had a drum and the child was duly imported, delighted to demonstrate his skill. Soon the garden throbbed to the drum beat of an early Beatle's song. Throb, throb – crash and bang. The cat remained unmoved.

At last people began to disperse. They had to get to bed and wishing us well, they shrugged and left. We had to get some sleep, too – except that for me it was to prove impossible. I went through the motions, letting the dog out, bolting the back door – that sort of thing. Beau settled onto his bed looking smug. Fancy getting stuck up a silly tree!

From our bedroom window that same tree, now a darkened mass, loomed like a ghostly presence out there with its unwilling occupant. I drew the curtains. Tomorrow would settle things, tomorrow a solution would be found. The night dragged slowly by and Bunting's cries, by now a little cracked, continued unabated. Finding it impossible to rest, we got up in the early hours and walked down the garden to the foot of that fateful tree and peered up through its thorny branches. There he was on the same branch and in the same desperate huddle. He looked as if all hope was lost – but upon seeing us inched forward as if he might jump. But it was not to be, for at the last moment his back legs slithered and upon regaining his balance he clung on with renewed frenzy to the branch that had become his prison. And then it came to me in a flash. I remembered how Beau had been dislodged with a gentle poke of the broom when he had wickedly embarked upon his siege of the tit box. Why not end Bunting's ordeal in the same way? It was so simple – so obvious.

By now the morning was well under way. Our neighbour again proffered his extended ladder and someone else arrived with a blanket to catch the animal when he fell. Then with steps in place, my husband armed with the garden broom, began his perilous ascent. A step higher and slowly another. Another step, a gentle shove and Bunting, as if jet propelled, hurtled to the ground! It happened in the blink of an eye and only just gave us time to position the blanket in time to land him like a large fish in a net.

No more yowls or piteous cries. Bunting blinked and, rather stunned, gazed around; and once indoors regained his equilibrium with remarkable rapidity – breakfasted heartily on his favourite sardines, and promptly curled up on his bed and went to sleep. Come that same evening there were no signs of the stresses to which he had been subjected. In no time at all he reverted to his usual placid and roly-poly self, unlike the rest of us upon whom the strains of the past twenty-four hours were more telling. His owners who were obliged to stagger through the following day worn out and weary.

Later we noticed something interesting. Bunting never again approached that particular tree and when in the garden with Beau, always gave it a wide berth and looked the other way should he need to pass it. There were other consequences, too. From then on he was to restrict his activities (never onerous) even more. He still enjoyed sunbathing, siestas and sardines out of a tin. But he never again looked at a butterfly and concentrated his energies, instead, upon ground based activities like catching earwigs and woodlice.

Never adventurous, or rarely so, Bunting's course was set, and from it he was seldom to deviate although, at times, he could surprise as will emerge later. Like Beau he, too, could behave "out of character", but then so can we all.

CHAPTER 11

Bunting's Secret World

Apparently, every morning at half past ten on the dot, Bunting had taken to leaving the safe haven of "his" flower pots to return promptly at midday looking mighty pleased with himself – his eyes bright as he danced homeward on the feline equivalent of tip-toe. This had been going on for several weeks before we noticed it, when one morning after gardening I was clearing up debris in the front garden and saw that he was not in his usual place. Neither was he there the next day, or the day after that: which was interesting but of little concern because he was always around, as usual, by tea time.

The days passed without incident, Bunting's absence noted and accepted with mild curiosity but that was all. Until one Monday when I was out walking Button (with Beau shadowing us as usual) and happened to meet a neighbour who owned the corner bungalow across the road. "I'm getting so fond of Bunting" she said. "I really miss him when it's time for him to go." I stared at her. "Time to go?" I queried. "Yes, every morning he comes to see Evangeline and then he disappears." Here a little explanation is necessary. Evangeline was Mrs Barber's Siamese cat. Of great beauty and extremely valuable, she had been bought as a house cat – far too precious to be let out – and introduced to us as a ten week old kitten. Fortunately for her, it had not been long before she had tasted freedom through an open window; and after

How do I get down?

that to keep her in had proved impossible, her vociferous protests being more than her kind hearted owner could bear.

So it was not to be long before she was climbing walls and fences before settling bolt upright like an anthracite statue on the pavement beyond the perimeter of the driveway. This was freedom too far and Mrs Barber had been distraught. The cat would get stolen, run over, squashed like an empty paper bag! Evangeline was instructed to confine herself to the limits of the back garden which, naturally, she ignored.

Until recently Evangeline's little life had been solitary, partly because of her fear and dislike of other cats; but she had been stoic in her loneliness and busy doing what she did best, which was to look beautiful. Until that is, one sunny day when along came Bunting. How had it happened? One can only guess. Presumably, from behind his pansies in their pots he had spied this beautiful creature and decided to investigate. Had crossed the Rubicon to make her acquaintance – and not been rebuffed!

They were an unlikely couple. One half, a neutered ginger tom descended from generations of alley cats – with a brimming brown eye, a sturdy step and a roly-poly figure. Who having been elevated from back streets to the leafy gardens of suburbia was now able to recognise real class when he saw it. The other half a haughty queen, daughter of Alfreda and sired by Percival 11, an award winning (first prize) veteran. What could she who was beauty personified, have seen in the tubby frame of our low bred moggie? Perhaps she admired his daring, or his good taste, or both?

Whatever the reason, from then on he had visited daily. She would wait for him on her piece of pavement and then withdraw with him to the back garden where, screened from prying eyes, they settled down to play. She would run round and round the lawn and he would trundle after her. She would stretch out beside the bird bath and he would follow suit and lie beside her. Then the real bonding began. She would lick the brow of his head and after a decent interval he would reciprocate by tending her ears. They rolled together, played hide and seek in the shrubbery until Mrs Barber rewarded them for their pains by offering a light lunch of freshly cooked plaice which they enjoyed side by side on her terrace.

Then, the repast finished, Evangeline would lead Bunting back into the front garden and should he hesitate, encourage him with a gentle nudge of her head in the direction of home. Surprisingly, she never attempted to cross the road with him but remained standing on the pavement until sure of his safe return behind his flower pots where he snoozed until it was time to rejoin Beau in our back garden. Only then did she return to settle on her square of pavement until, come time, and much to her owner's delight, she was moved to return indoors.

In astonishment I listened to this tale of feline romance and was delighted with her admiration of our pet, "so friendly and so beautifully marked." Briefly and in an instant, Bunting the timid had become Bunting the daring who had been enjoying a secret and rewarding, other life. Had shown determination and initiative sufficient for us from now on, to regard him with new eyes.

It was a charming state of affairs and one in which the proud owners on both sides of the divide were to delight; but not for long for, sadly, fairy tale endings in real life are rare and this was not to turn out to be one of them.

CHAPTER 12

Hand of Fate

As things turned out, Bunting and Evangeline were only to continue their friendship for a matter of weeks. They did not know it but they were living on borrowed time and how sad it was that this true tale was to end prematurely and unhappily. For no sooner had the cats established their delightful routine than fate dealt a cruel hand. Evangeline was plucked from this life and suddenly and inexplicably Bunting's lady love was no more.

At the time she was only eighteen months old and had appeared well and happy. But on that fateful day she ate her evening meal for the last time, keeled over, gave a frightened gasp; a sound Mrs Barber said that was a cross between a sigh and a scream…… and breathed her last.

Our neighbour was distraught. The vet was sent for, pronounced the cat dead and suggested an autopsy which was duly carried out. In the meantime rumours circulated. Rat poison was suggested and an accusing finger pointed at next door's gardener who had been heard to complain of "damage" and in the same breath, "foxes!"……

Or perhaps she had been hit by a car and had died from internal injuries? A young man had been seen speeding, using the road "like a race track." A young man who had not had the decency to come forward and own up. Perhaps…. Perhaps. Rumour and counter rumour, but in the end it was revealed that Evangeline had died from natural causes, a massive cerebral haemorrhage. There had been no hint that she was in anything but the best of health and we were all very sad.

The next morning Bunting stretched, flexed his muscles and combed his whiskers prior to vacating his pansy pots for his daily visit to his lady friend. She was not sitting on the corner to greet him. Nonplussed, he wandered round into the back garden – to the lawn, the scene of so many happy gambols. She was not there, but the scent of her was.

Where could she be? Carefully, he checked every plant and investigated dark corners. Nothing. Back he went into the front where he inspected her patch of pavement, the garden wall and the path up to her front door. No sign – no hint of her in the flesh, just her scent everywhere and the memories…. Then he sat down and howled, out there on the pavement; an eerie primitive sound which invaded the quiet road and garden like a supernatural visitation.

Mrs Barber opened her front door and let him in where he searched and searched: under the beds, behind the chairs, in every corner and cranny until, finally, in the kitchen where Evangeline was fed and there was still no evidence of her, he began once more to howl. So she rang me up and begged me to go round and fetch him, for in her own wounded state that dreadful sound was both unsettling and disquieting. Over I went and picked him up. His usually relaxed and tubby little body was taut and knotted, and as we crossed the road for home he gazed at me with large amber eyes that registered misery and incomprehension.

Cats cannot cry because they do not have the physical means to do so. But they can show distress. Bunting's eyes were glazed, his whiskers drooped and no sooner was he home than he struggled to return to the bungalow in order to continue the fruitless search. So it went on day after day – after day. He would not eat and he lost weight. He howled, but gradually the periods in between lengthened and then it stopped: although for weeks he still spent his mornings fruitlessly searching.

Eventually, it was an Evangeline Mark 2 who saved the day. Bought in the teeth of opposition by a daughter concerned at her mother's grief, Anastasia, a Siamese kitten with wide eyes and wobbly legs, won everybody's heart – even Bunting's.

He still continued to search, but now with less rigour and it was not long before he started to take a proud and avuncular interest in the new kitten. His life regained its earlier rhythm and his tubby placidity returned. In the early morning it was again garden patrol with Beau. Then before retreating to his flower pots, he would play nurse and nanny to Anastasia, who, like her predecessor, took to waiting for him in the front garden. As before, he never outstayed his welcome and before leaving would indulge with her in a saucer of milk before setting off for home.

CHAPTER 13

The "Cat Lady" Again

It seemed so long ago since Beau had been collected from the "cat lady" and Bunting rescued from a watery grave. It was, in fact, a little over two years since Bunting's arrival which meant that our white cat had been with us for just over three. But it might as well have been three hundred for time is deceptive and now it was impossible to imagine what life had been like without them.

We had on occasion, discussed the "cat lady", wondering if she were still doing her rescue work, but had seen no more of her advertisements in the local press which raised the possibility that she had gone out of business. But as we were soon to find out this was most definitely not the case.

However, when the phone rang one evening, and the caller identified herself as Jo Jo's good Samaritan, I was at first at a loss; and then in a flash the memory of that eventful visit which had been the starting point of Beau's new life returned. I remembered him being lifted by the scruff of his neck and squirted, back and front, with anti flea powder. As if on a spool of newsreel, it all came back, and most importantly, I remembered his earlier name Bo Bo! Of course, this was the "cat lady" on the telephone.

As things turned out, Mrs Proctor, for that was her real name, was still very much involved with her cat rescue work. She was going to be in our area, visiting one of her "placements" as she called them and wondered if she might call and see how "Bo Bo" was getting on? So this was how she came to be invited to tea, at a time when Beau would put in an appearance, as he always did – for his saucer of milk. Or nearly always.

But life is uncertain, and animals, like children, do not always perform as we would like. Mrs Proctor duly arrived and parked her car on our drive. Where else would she park it? An obvious question, but the point is that our cat would have both seen and heard her arrival. Was this why he chose not to conform to his usual routine? Or was there some other reason? For conform he did not! Tea and biscuits came and went, the minutes ticked by but Beau was nowhere to be seen. We duly apologised.

We called him... and called! We walked outside and searched for him in all his favourite places, by the pool, among the roses, in the shrubbery. Mrs Proctor admired the garden, but it was clear that she would soon have to leave and without her mission accomplished. Back indoors more refreshment was proffered but all eyes kept straying to the garden. Beau had vanished, but in his stead Bunting padded in and plopped down on our "cat lady's" knee. She admired him.

We began to feel a trifle foolish. Perhaps Mrs Proctor would become suspicious, begin to imagine that Beau had not been provided with the requisite "loving home" after all? Perhaps our cat (whose neck by now, I would willingly have rung) had got himself locked in the garden shed? It was investigated and he had not. So we had to content ourselves by recounting in his absence, how our white cat had grown into one of the most beautiful, intelligent and home loving of pets – but it all began to ring a little hollow. Where was he?

After a while it was time for our "cat lady" to leave. She had another appointment, was disappointed but perhaps some other time...? Bunting was discharged from her knee and she was shown to the front door when suddenly she remembered that she had left her purse on the arm of her chair where she had been sitting. Geoffrey went back into the room to retrieve it and there, to his amazement, curled up on her vacated seat was Beau, looking for all the world as though he had been there for hours! His pink nose was encircled by his magnificent tail, his eyes closed as he lay relaxed and oblivious of all human kind.

That is how we came to return hurriedly into the room where we stood for a few seconds, speechless. Mrs Proctor was the first to speak. "Cats," she said were "mavericks" which was part of their charm. Maybe, but on this occasion he was not charming me! Our visitor was encouraged to sit down again and pick Beau up. He rolled placidly on his back and, gently purring, waved his paws in the air. Then he opened an eye and I could swear that had he been human, it would have been a wink. He invited Mrs Proctor to tickle his stomach, performed his "roll over" act and fluffed up his coat to look like ermine.

At last, having praised, pampered and pondered upon the vagaries of cats in general, our "cat lady" finally took her leave – clearly impressed with the feline prodigy into which our little stray kitten had grown. There were smiles all round.

When we had waved Mrs Proctor goodbye, we sat back and looked at each other. Where had Beau been? Why had he ignored our repeated appeals and what on earth had he been doing? At once the concept of parallel lives sprang to mind. It is one, with which all cats are familiar and which, from time to time, drives cat owners to distraction. For cats live on two planes at the same time. The domestic one with their owner who is permitted to care for them – provide food, warmth, shelter and affection. The other, a secret, feral existence which encourages them to scent and hunt and mark their territory; an alien territory, unpeopled by humans and eons old.

Sometimes the planes overlap and when they do it is the domestic one that must give way. This is what might explain Beau's behaviour, for as it turned out, he had been in the living room with us all the time. He had heard us calling and it had meant little, for he had been behind the settee with the remains of an unfortunate field mouse. His mood had been the feline equivalent of "not at home" and until the business in hand had been despatched, he did not want to know.

Come the evening, however, he was again his old self, had re-entered our world with a flourish; his return well signposted as he climbed onto laps, nuzzled his head and filled the room with the rumble of his purr.

CHAPTER 14

Stranger Cat

There was tension in the air. An intruder had entered the garden and at first Beau could not believe his eyes. He froze – watched and waited from his vantage point up in the apple tree. Oblivious, the uninvited visitor strolled nonchalantly across the terrace, peered into the fish pond before setting off to explore the garden, ignoring the "keep off" warnings that had been sprayed upon bush and brier with such care that morning. The interloper browsed among the roses, showed (from Beau's point of view) an unhealthy interest in one of the dog's bones before, horror of horrors, he ended up beneath the umbrella of our white cat's apple tree! The latter's eyes were like skewers as slowly, very slowly indeed, he inched his way down to take control. It was the final leap that gave the game away and by the time he was positioned to confront the stranger cat the latter was already alerted.

Now both animals froze. Then, their heads turned sideways, their ears back, they began to circle. Beau gave his war cry, a high pitched shriek which usually encouraged a quick retreat. Undaunted, stranger cat responded in kind and it would seem that we were in for quite a spectacle as round and round the two gyrated in preparation for the "battle" to follow.

The intruder was heavier than Beau. Sleek and black he was well fed and pumped up for a scrap. Our cat was the wiry one. Lithe and agile, his toughness was not apparent. He was a small cat, his muscles stacked beneath his long haired coat of brilliant white. But what he lacked in size he made up for with intent. He was very angry – his patch had been invaded – and fired up he attacked. His claw missed his opponent's eye but split his nose. Stranger cat's response was to slice Beau's ear (an ear which bore the scar to the end of his life) and rip the side of his face.

Soon one lost count. The action quickened: claws, teeth and flying fur. Stranger cat was proving a problem. The shrieks and yowls reached a crescendo and were beginning to attract attention. Windows opened. Then just as we were debating about intervention before the animals killed each other, Bunting did it for us! Awoken from sweet dreams he emerged from his usual hide away to peep timidly around the side door and see what was going on. What he saw was Beau in trouble and astonishingly and without hesitation – he joined in. Placid and portly, forget all that. Timid and unadventurous, forget that too….

Now the fact was that stranger cat could not fight on two fronts at the time. While his teeth and claws were busy in front his hindquarters were vulnerable. So it was in that direction that our ginger tom cat sprang, sinking his claws and teeth into the animal's rear. At last and with a final howl stranger cat was forced to let go of his grip on Beau and drag himself off. He was in a sorry state, had had enough and was now more concerned with getting away than with "finishing off" his opponent. Which was just as well for, by now, both cats were bleeding profusely and our white cat's pristine white was matted with blood.

Then as suddenly as he had attacked, Bunting sprang back and away to wherever he had come from: no doubt in case he might become the next target. Which left Beau alone, a fallen hero with blood streaming from a slit nose and jagged left ear. Or nearly alone for there were always his fans on hand to encourage and cosset him after he had summoned the strength to crawl into the kitchen and be bathed, and at last to fall into an exhausted sleep on his bed.

We never saw stranger cat in our garden again – but later I did see him sunning himself on his own front law, recovered and resplendent. As for Beau? Even before his scars were healed he had convinced himself of victory and was correspondingly jaunty. Later when completely recovered he was to wear his battle scars like medals. For did they not serve as a deterrent to others? Did they not signal him to be a doughty fighter – one who must always be respected?

CHAPTER 15

Cat and Mouse

Like most cats Beau was interested in mousing. Or to put it another way, for a considerable period of his young life it was to become an abiding passion. On these hunting expeditions he was often sighted in woods several miles from home; or more frequently in our garden or a neighbour's, nosing his way through long grass before spurting into a run which culminated in the inevitable pounce. As a gesture of goodwill he would then present his "trophies" to me, leaving them in unexpected places in the living room – so that when one was groping for a book, for example, or a pen under the settee one would find, instead, a pathetic little corpse. Or he would leave them in the kitchen as a hint, perhaps, as to what might be done with them. It was not a "hobby" of which I approved: was one I would have liked to prevent which was usually impossible, although there were rare instances when human cunning prevailed.

One Saturday morning was just such an example. It was early in the day and Beau had "bagged" his quarry and carried the little creature onto our back lawn where he crouched, his live prey between his paws, feigning boredom as he looked around or gazed skyward until his hapless prisoner made a desperate bid for freedom. But it was all a cruel ploy and cat and captive were soon back as before with the baby mouse only safe so long as it played "dead". By now the two were nearing the kitchen window in readiness for the whole pathetic little drama to be played out again. Cat gazed up to Heaven, mouse scuttled away to be caught and brought back as before.

It was all too near for comfort and I determined to act; but how and in what way? To call Beau, or worse, to approach him would be useless for he would run away, taking his unfortunate victim with him. To offer him an alternative, food that he especially liked, had been tried before to no avail. So something else had to be done and done quickly before our cat became bored with his cruel little game and put an end to it.

From a drawer in the writing desk I found the binoculars and trained them upon jailor and captive. The latter turned out to be a young harvest mouse, plump and with wide ears. It was still very much alive. Its eyes were open and its coat sleek – a beautiful specimen that had not yet died of fright so there was still hope, although common sense dictated that the battle must be nearly lost.

In a flash I had an idea! Create a counter disturbance. Distract Beau's attention and allow time for a little manoeuvre. I went into the kitchen and from a cupboard extracted a large transparent pudding basin. Thus armed, I ventured via the back door into the garden a good distance from where the cat was crouching. Then I picked up a handful of pebbles and headed for the back lawn.

Beau watched my approach keenly – and I knew that to venture too near would be the signal for him to run off and take "his" mouse with him. So now was the time for reassurance, a demonstration that I had no "evil" intent.

"What a good boy" I cooed, feeling a hypocrite. "What a clever boy."

Beau resumed his study of the heavens. A quick glance down at his captive and that was all. I ventured a little closer. Beau's paws still encircled the mouse but now they were relaxed, his pads bland. One step too close, however, and all would change. With bayonet claws and scissor teeth off into the shrubbery he would rush with another soon-to-be dead harvest mouse to add to the ever growing list.

So I stopped and threw my first handful of pebbles, causing noise and a splattering of movement beyond his immediate field of vision, behind some tall plants. Then I finished up with a number of larger stones which each landed with a thud in roughly the same direction. Beau's interest was aroused. The pebbles encouraged him to look for movement and the repeated thuds of the stones determined him to investigate. Leaving his prey he set off in the direction of the disturbances which meant that it was now time to further my plan with speedy action. I pounced and managed to cover the terrified and temporarily discarded mouse with my transparent, upside down pudding basin.

But all was not yet over, for Act Two was to prove more difficult than might be imagined. How to get the mouse safely out of his prison and away? First Beau must be caught and carried indoors for as long as was necessary;

Relaxing in the sunshine.

and that was to prove no easy task. By now he was furious. He knew that he had been duped and was determined that a trick like that was not going to happen again. On sentry duty he guarded his mouse in its transparent prison, only to run away at the moment anybody tried to catch him: and to attempt to remove the latter with the cat in such close proximity was too risky.

Time passed and the sun came out. The basin was covered with a cloth to prevent it overheating as heat exhaustion was not on the agenda.

Eventually it became clear that our pet must be frightened away. So he was shooed out of the way by the brandishing of a folded newspaper. He was soon to return, only to find that the mouse had gone, eased gently into a cardboard box, marched up the road and released in nearby woods. There it scuttled away and I trust lived out its lifespan without any more trauma.

Back home, Beau was on duty again beside the now empty basin. No doubt it still smelt of mouse and comforted him with the thought of what might have been – but on this occasion at least – was not. For some time he studiously ignored me. I had betrayed and belittled him and no self respecting cat could be expected to put up with that. And he just could not figure out where the mouse had gone….

But as supper time approached, he was tempted to sink his pride. He came into the kitchen for his food, and with Bunting at his side, ate an enormous meal. Not long after we were again friends, an understanding arrived at when he graciously determined to sit upon my knee.

CHAPTER 16

Highs and Lows

It was a bright June morning and Button and I prepared for our usual walk. On went her lead and off we went, me with a smile and she with a wag of her tail.

We had gone about half a mile when I noticed what appeared to be a white paper bag in the middle of a flower bed in a front garden. As we approached it moved and upon closer inspection, turned out to be Beau. Often in the past Beau had taken a few tentative steps with us along our way, but had always turned back and skipped off home when the going got tough. This time it was different. We had already navigated several roads and the cat seemed inclined to stay with us. I was in a hurry which meant that to try and catch him (impossible anyway) or to turn back, would take as long as to carry on. After all, on hunting expeditions Beau was known to have braved traffic and travelled miles; and was he not also a seasoned siesta taker in the middle of our lane? Things would work out, I hoped.

So we developed a routine. When we got level with him the cat dashed on ahead, threading his way through gardens and behind hedges with obvious enjoyment. So the three of us proceeded; the dog as carefree as a cloud, the cat in pixie mode and their owner, by now, a trifle nervous. Along our route a lady opened an upstairs window. "Excuse me" she called out, "but is that a cat you have with you?"

"Yes" I responded, endeavouring to sound as if walking a cat was the most natural thing to do. "Oh" came the reply, "I thought it was" and she promptly banged the window shut to re-emerge in the front garden to take a closer look. Beau ran off. "You've lost it" she cried; and somehow Beau being referred to as an "it" was mildly offensive.

Button and I continued our walk. We arrived at a crossroads (still no Beau) and entered a little wood – an area as familiar to me as breakfast cereal. But today I did not hear the bird song or take time out to admire the green canopy overhead. Instead I was too busy deciding where we would site our "Have you seen this cat?" posters.

The wood led to the common from where we would turn right for home. Button realising that something was wrong turned back to walk closely beside me and together we made a miserable pair. Then, just as we were about to leave the wooded area there was a scuffle high up in a tree above us and out fell Beau all claws and tail! As we were now about a mile and a half from home and I had more or less given up finding our pet, I was ecstatic – and at the same time furious with him for worrying me in this way. I grabbed him and, amazingly, managed to catch hold of his tail. He gave a loud, protesting yowl – was very angry, so that made two of us. Transferring my grip from his tail to the scruff of his neck, I carried him home. Usually so feather light, Beau was now a dead weight. My arms ached and I vowed never again to set out without making sure that he was safely locked indoors. But we made it! And the relief as he tumbled unceremoniously from my grip and into the hall was exquisite, if short lived. Beau was furious. He glared, he spat and shot out of the kitchen window to disappear into the shrubbery at the bottom of the garden.

For the rest of the day there was no sign of him. Meal times came and went. Bunting arrived on the dot for both dinner and supper, munching away contentedly, and as night fell took up his usual position on my knee, facing the door for a quick get-away if needed. No Beau. We called and called, gave up and settled down to read. Then our apparent lack of concern was rewarded. For an hour later, a wail like the siren sound of a banshee rent the flimsy dark. It was coming from the garden room where, pressed against the patio door, was the spectre of a white cat – a pale ghost outlined against the deepening night, a ghost with an offering in its mouth. One that was very much alive – an owlet which fluttered on fledgling wings.

So was one problem succeeded by another. The little creature must be saved; but in attempting this we would be rejecting a peace offering. Undaunted, we set to work. First of all doors and windows were closed. Then, as the baby bird was gently extricated from Beau's clamped jaws, a bowl of chicken liver was thrust instead under his nose. The liver proved a successful foil for the cat was ravenous. Soon his face was swimming above the food and the owlet safe in a box preparatory to being released.

The liver demolished, we told our cat how grateful we were for his gift. We stroked him, tickled his chin and soon with an overly distended stomach, he was lying snoring on the rug. Now and again he opened an eye, rolled over for a tickle. Then he punched the air with the pads of his upturned paws before succumbing again to the deep and dreamless sleep of those without a care.

He had forgiven, he had forgotten. Life was back to normal. At least it was for our white cat but not yet quite for me. And this is where animals are fortunate. They live for the moment whereas humans find this more difficult. We remember and we worry.

CHAPTER 17

Winners don't Wash

Bunting had got something and Beau wanted it. From behind the sofa came scuffling sounds, scratching and an amalgam of other cat noises not so easily identifiable. Alert in a comfy chair, Beau's ears were pricked, monitoring and unscrambling – making sense of what to us were just the noises of a cat at play.

It was a cold winter evening and our animals had both been lying quietly on the same chair, limbs entwined, enjoying the warm indoors after the briefest of spells outside. To get them in the garden at all they had had to be cajoled – even bullied a little. Then, no sooner out than two pathetic little faces appeared, pressed against the patio window, begging to be allowed back inside.

Bunting had recently gone through a phase when he refused point blank to remove himself from our house on a rainy day unless accompanied by an upheld umbrella! Astonished neighbours watched the performance as he squatted down under cover before racing back to the warmth of the fire. One, choking with laughter, admitted that he had been unable to believe his eyes and indeed it was sheer pantomime quickly forgotten as rain turned to watery shine and the animal came to his senses.

But to return indoors and to that winter evening. It had been peaceful. The two cats asleep in an embrace and Button in sole charge of the hearthrug. She was snoring and dreaming, her nose twitching as she emitted little yelps of excitement, chasing imaginary rabbits down the byways of her mind. Then it was "all change". Bunting awoke and without more ado, strode purposefully out of the room. We took no notice. Button and Beau continued to sleep off the rigours of another "busy" day. Neither did we take notice when our red cat returned – not to the shared chair with Beau, but to a more private place behind the settee. It was then that the noises started. Clearly, he was playing with something. Was it yet another mouse to be rescued? Was it a toy or something of more value? The noises grew louder; then Beau's nose began to twitch, his ears pricked and he decided to investigate. Down he jumped and approached the settee. This signalled a change in the "off stage" sounds that we had been getting. Now the scuffling and scratching was replaced by a growl – a continuous warning growl, signalling "keep off"! Knowing Bunting as we did, it was hard to believe that our placid, portly and sweet tempered red cat could care about anything sufficiently to warn off his more determined and streetwise "brother". But on this occasion, clearly he did care and we could only deduce that what he had was of great importance to him. Which was all very well, except that if it mattered to Bunting it was also, now his interest was aroused, going to matter to Beau.

Behind the settee more was going on. Bunting's growls became translated into shrieks; and bumps and bangs increased both in volume and number. At last it all became too much and still with his prized possession in his mouth, out rushed our red cat to take refuge in the kitchen. It was to prove a false move. Behind the settee, Beau's movements and options had been limited but now out in the open he was free to go into action – which he did!

And it did not take him long to vanquish his opponent who by then was reduced to a marmalade pulp. So it was that the victor, his jaws clamped tight and his tail held high, shot out of the room to investigate and enjoy his prize in private where he might savour the full flavour of victory uninterrupted by prying eyes and disapproving comments. Where did he end up? One might have guessed it: back behind and under the sofa of course from where the growling started up again but in a different key and from a different throat.

It is an event hardly worth recording except for the ultimate outcome, which all must agree added a mix of humour to the proceedings. First Bunting returned to the living room and after a thorough wash, a routine followed by all embarrassed cats, settled down happily again on a knee: then Beau emerged, his jaws unclamped and mouth empty, not to wash, winners don't wash, but to unpack himself in front of the fire.

No sign of the trophy. Had it run away or been returned to where it was found? Had it been eaten or was it still there, sneaked under the settee? We couldn't resist a quick peep and what we found was to provide us with a tale to dine out on for days to come. There, discarded and beneath contempt, wounded with teeth and claw marks, was of all things the remains of a vegetarian sausage of the type that had been served up for supper the previous night. All that fuss over a meat-free sausage. Could it be that after so many years our cats were ready to embark upon a vegetarian diet? Or was it all an unfortunate mistake?

All I can report is that both animals tucked into their evening meal of rabbit casserole (which is what it said on the tin) with great enthusiasm; and that later still they lay down together to sleep it off without a hint of rancour.

Another day, another "adventure" in the lives of our two cats.

CHAPTER 18

A New Experience

One winter's day a stoat arrived in our garden with a white coat as beautiful as the one that Beau wore. But there the similarity ended, for this strange creature was used to fending for itself, something that our feline friends could only pretend to do. Having escaped captivity, our new arrival had reverted to the wild; was an expert predator with razor sharp teeth and claws to match.

Beau did not like what he saw and I prepared myself for a re-run of the stranger cat episode with some trepidation. Our white cat was a poor loser and in any case I did not want him hurt. The stoat, like so many wild animals, was a creature of habit. It arrived each morning on the dot of half past ten to spend precious moments lurking in our pet's favourite places – the rose bed or around the mouse nest under the garden shed.

This gave Beau time to contemplate his next move. He knew that Bunting could be discounted; for darling though he was, as fighting went he was just plain yellow with the guts of a wood louse. Although he could surprise as has been seen.

Day upon day Beau watched the intruder making free with "his" property; sunning himself beneath Beau's apple tree, foraging among his nasturtiums, sniffing around his goldfish pool and, worst of all, gobbling greedily the bird food which our cat enjoyed to steal as a divine right!

It was to bring back memories of his earlier confrontations with Boss Cat and Stranger Cat – experiences which he was loath to repeat. However the day arrived when action could be postponed no longer. When Beau, pumped up and fluffed out waited, crouched behind a rose bush for the "enemy" to approach. Which on the dot he did, swaggering across the lawn without a care in the world.

Perhaps after the Stranger Cat episode, our pet was determined to re-assert himself; perhaps he felt it was now or never. Or perhaps he simply hadn't learnt his lesson. So, emitting his usual shriek, Beau went into the attack, expecting immediate flight. He did not get it. Instead he was to feel the full impact of teeth and claws which ripped and scratched….. until bleeding and battered he staggered back into the house, leaving the "enemy" to continue playing "king of the castle" outside.

We bathed his wounds; we were getting used to that. But he was very shaken, refusing food and apparently unable or unwilling to get up from his bed. A visit to the vet was in order. One which cheered him a little because he was the centre of attention. Antibiotics were prescribed in case of infection and home we came where again he relapsed into lethargy and gloom. Even so, with the aid of a veterinary "shot gun" we managed to propel the pills down his throat in a battle of wills which we hoped would result in some signs of recovery.

In the meantime and to make matters even worse, it was clear that Bunting and our stoat were getting along just fine. For the former made no attempt to "discipline" the latter and seemed content to share our garden with this stranger without demure. Fish pond, mouse nest, apple tree, it was all the same to Bunting, especially as the visitor after his decisive victory over Beau, was content to keep his teeth and claws to himself. Even more unbelievable, the two animals were sometimes seen sharing a common patch of sunlight on the lawn.

Soon Beau's physical wounds were healed but his mental trauma persisted and it was clear that we had returned to his state of mind at the time of the

Boss Cat episode. So it was with a distinct sense of déjà vu that we watched our white cat as he sat for hours behind the patio window, refusing to venture out yet unable to tear himself away from watching the stoat as it made free with Bunting in our garden.

The "Boss Cat" affair had solved itself. It will be remembered that cat and owner had moved away. But this was different. There was no owner, or at least only one from which the animal had presumably escaped. So the days rolled by as hour upon hour Beau was to be seen "alone and palely loitering", a mere shadow of his former, robust self behind his glass prison. He lost weight, his tail drooped and his condition deteriorated so badly that yet another visit to the vet was deemed necessary.

"Stoats" he said "are nocturnal animals" as he listened to our tale of woe with incredulity. "Not this one" I replied "and what is more Bunting seems perfectly happy to have it around." More discussion and a plan of action unfolded but only after Mr Robson had seen the animal for himself. He duly arrived and was offered coffee. Then as he stared out onto our lawn where our intruder was enjoying a "siesta" in a patch of sunlight, confirmed that the animal we were playing unwilling host to was, indeed, a stoat. Neither he nor we could understand Bunting's apparently happy involvement with the animal, but we could all see the effect that the situation was having on Beau. Beau who by now was almost skeletal, because he could or would not take time out from his window gazing to eat, which in turn served to increase his feelings of hopelessness and helplessness.

Mr Robson returned to his car and from the boot extracted a cat trap of the kind that was used to entice feral cats and introduce them to good homes. Wearing gloves we were advised to bait the cage with food and place it where there was plenty of cover. Then we waited…… and waited. The days passed, the food remained untouched and the trap empty. Still our "guest" was much in evidence; here and there and up and down the garden which was now quite clearly regarded as home. To make matters worse, Button, our Labrador, had decided to change sides and throw in her lot with Bunting and the enemy.

After a brief skirmish, a scratch and a fright, she had come to see our stoat as an unfortunate reality to be endured, the creature was only aggressive if confronted.

Then one morning we noticed that the trapdoor of the device was shut; and as at that moment there appeared to be no sign of the stoat we were jubilant – approached the device to get a better look at what was inside.

The contraption had worked perfectly and with guillotine-like precision. But nonetheless we were in for a shock! For imagine our dismay when we found that we had caught – not the intruder but our own much loved and greedy Bunting; who far from being frightened by his experience was still happily munching away!

As it was, he was let out, showing a noticeable reluctance for freedom because there was still some food left inside; was carried protesting indoors to avoid a repeat performance. Then the trap was reset and this time our ploy was successful. It still took time. Two days and nights; but on the following Friday morning we found our prey, gnashing his teeth but safe inside with the guillotine door firmly down.

It had already been decided what to do with him. He would be taken to woodland where he would find food and shelter and released: far away from our garden, out of sight and out of mind. And that is what we did.

Fortunately the stoat did not return and for Beau a slow recovery began. He continued to look and look, but when it gradually became clear that there was now no enemy outside either lurking or cavorting, he managed, with much encouragement, a few shaky turns around the terrace. Then he ate a desultory mouthful of dinner and the following day even managed a brief snooze in the sun.

Improvement accelerated. By the end of the week he felt sufficiently strong to take his early constitutional around the garden, marking his territory. It was an activity that had been sadly neglected, because without the white cat's example, it had never entered Bunting's head to carry on the tradition. But now as before, he was quick to fall in line behind.

Beau soon regained the weight he had lost and his magnificent tail became again the banner that it once was. The nightmare was over and in a surprisingly short time he was, as before, the captain of his own ship, or rather top cat in his own garden. At least for a while.

CHAPTER 19

A Chance Encounter

One day Beau was skittering along the top of "his" fence, when he met another cat coming in the opposite direction. This was going to be interesting because our pet's dislike of other cats was only matched by his affection for us – the two ends so as to speak, of a see-saw. So as there was no way that either animal could continue along its precarious way unless the other gave way, and as Beau was seldom defeated, we expected the encounter to be over quickly; the intruder to be downed, despatched within seconds and our white cat with his territorial rights restored, to continue breezily along his way.

Not a bit of it! Events were to prove us wrong and illustrate that our understanding of our pet was not as complete as we complacently had thought. This new cat on the block was young, black and sleek except for a fleck of white at the tip of her tail. She was dainty – very dainty, which was why I presumed her to be female, a deduction that was to prove correct and which undoubtedly influenced what was to follow.

Beau puffed up and stood his ground, but did not attack. There was no demon shriek, no tight ball of feline fury. The little black cat was stopped in her tracks. She had got the message, indeed she could not have missed it and she responded, not by jumping down, but by subsiding with head bowed into a submissive crouch: and so, as if posed for a painting, that was how they remained, frozen in time. Neither moved, the younger cat paralysed with fear, the elder most certainly not although he was undecided how to proceed.

He remained at a loss. To attack such a pitiful little creature seemed unnecessary for she had already submitted, but there was no getting away from the fact that his right of way was still blocked. Looked at from one angle he had won – from another he had not. So he did what all cats do when they are embarrassed or uncertain of what to do next. He began to wash himself, no easy task on top of a six foot high fence. Then he sniffed the "intruder" and fluffed up a tad more as she crouched even lower.

Our white cat made a decision. Without a hint of aggression he lightly jumped over the frightened animal in his path to land half on and half off the fence on the other side of her, pulling himself up to regain his balance with a fair bit of slithering and slipping. One might then have expected him to continue along his way, but he did not; and as the object of his attention remained inert and submissive, continued to finish the sniffing operation begun earlier.

Then he jumped down, the better to gaze up at her from the ground until sometime later the little cat at last raised herself, braced to glance down. Their eyes met. For moments neither moved until Beau at last decided to cement the fragility of their relationship by adopting his I- want- to- play pose, rolling on his back and waving all four paws in the air.

More time passed… until little black cat, oh so slowly raised herself sufficiently to slither down to the ground where she was greeted by Beau with a couple of licks to the forehead. Tentatively she responded, nestling her nose against Beau's left ear, a gesture well received because it was not to be long before the two of them were playing hide-and-seek in the shrubbery at the bottom of the garden. A pact had been made, a friendship forged.

At the same time the next day Beau mounted his fence to sit sentinel – watching and waiting for the little black cat to arrive which she very soon did, eager to meet up again with her new friend. This time our pet was not pumped up, just a little fluffed to create a good impression: and with his banner of a tail, a gleam in his eye and a cocked cockle-shell ear, this was not difficult. Neither was it a problem for Mitzi (for that was her name) as when she made her entrance she was as different from her former self as a butterfly from a chrysalis. Now she danced her way, perky as a pixie, along to their appointed meeting. Then the two rubbed noses and both sprang down to embark upon their business for the day: to play catch-as-catch-can or hide-and-seek again forever, or until they tired.

After this the two were to meet frequently, usually when Bunting was safely over the road, paying his respects to Evangeline. Unlike Evangeline, Mitzi was no aristocrat – just a pretty little "moggie" who had recently come to live a few doors away. But who cared? Beau certainly did not. For to him she was as beautiful as the most pampered and expensive of felines – she was a star.

Apart from Bunting, Mitzi was the only cat that our pet would ever tolerate in his garden. This was different. This was a "friendship" that was to last for the rest of his life and when many, many years later Beau was to leave us, Mitzi was as inconsolable as Bunting had been when Evangeline died.

CHAPTER 20

Indoor Games

It was another grey day; windy with squally showers and the cats were bored. They would not venture outside for wet paws, as always, were unacceptable; so instead they sat, hunched with disapproval on any spare chair they could find. And there could be no forgetting who they blamed for destroying their outdoor fun. It was me! I had sent the wind and I had somehow "magicked" the rain, deliberately to prevent their usual feline pleasures: such as exploring the wild wasteland under the hedge, or lurking behind the woodshed to rustle up a spider or two, or tease a magnificent stag beetle back, double quick, into the dark crevasse from where it came.

Like bored children they were bent on trouble. They tried chasing their own tails round and round in a giddy whirl; then they chased each other's which turned out badly because they soon forgot it was a game and started nipping as well until squeaks and squeals destroyed the morning peace.

But, thank goodness, even that palled when a new idea took hold. It began with pages of the Sunday newspaper inadvertently left around on the floor. At first, a little nip here and there which, once they got the taste for it, quickly turned into vandalising long strips of the stuff. Soon whole pages were shredded and our Sunday trip to the newsagent a waste of time. That was when we decided to take action: to banish them from the living room and shut the door on them in the study upstairs. If they were going to sulk then let them do it out of sight and out of harm's way.

This was how a new game came into being – rain drop catching or rather tracing. Through a glass door on the landing we saw them playing, so intent that they took no heed of footsteps nor even of dinner time as that usually eagerly awaited hour approached. Our cats were sociable and friendly creatures but now, like gamblers hooked on horse racing, or dice throwers intent around a gaming table, they were oblivious of anything except the frankly impossible task that they had set themselves. For how does one "catch" a raindrop?

This was how the game was played. Both cats sat like a couple of book ends, back to back on the side sill beneath the bay widow. It has been raining hard and they had first been attracted by the sound of pattering and the occasional splatter of water against the glass. Indeed, the more the rain splashed and sloshed the more interested they became. The fiercer the storm outside the more intently they looked and listened. And then the rain subsided a little: not much but sufficiently for individual drops to be traced from where they first made contact with the top of the glass, down to their final resting place at the bottom and then off, disappearing into the moist air. Each cat would "fix" upon the droplet of his choice. To get a close view this involved standing up on hind legs; then with a front paw outstretched, the rain drop would be covered with a bland pad that traced its watery descent towards the window's limit.

Sometimes the descent was clear and straight, but often it was not, meandering a little here and there like a microscopic rivulet. Then the challenge required was greater and so was the concentration, as in a series of balletic moves paws moved a little this way and that intent upon ensuring that all was not lost in the infinite watery blur that the window had become. It was an arduous task, for no sooner had one rain drop been safely shepherded "home" than another took its place!

With so much work to be done, our cats even forgot their supper. On and on they played until it grew dark and then they curled up and fell asleep on the wide window sill with their tails bandages around their eyes and noses to indicate that they were not to be disturbed. So our evening progressed with no more interruptions. What was left of the newspaper was read and then discarded, with some relief, for we had come round to the belief that there was so little of interest in its pages that perhaps our cats had been right after all when they embarked upon ripping it up.

At bedtime two cats, heavy with sleep and dead to the world, were transferred to their baskets downstairs. Beside each bed was placed a full supper dish which elicited no response from either of them.

But by morning the rain had stopped and the bowls were empty. Beau was raring to get on with the business of the day – no thought of raindrops now. And as for Bunting? Well, the flower pots were waiting and he was ready......

Time for a snack. Bunting tucks in.

CHAPTER 21

Water, Water

Beau had been fishing; had spent hours cradling his chin over the brim of the pond, tracking our five gold fish as they glided round and round. There used to be ten of them, which says a good deal about his expertise in this field but now, protected by netting, the remainder continued to provide ongoing entertainment and temptation.

Then as one of the larger fish, a claw's breadth from death, glinted beneath his dangling paw Beau pounced, tipped over the edge to bounce onto the netting and become entangled. Down he sank and as the netting bulged, surfaced spluttering, his coat darkly soggy and his tail, his beautiful tail, rat like. So he struggled and struggled some more, each time becoming more desperate to escape.

By the time I realised what had happened and hurried to help, our cat was exhausted and in distress. By then he was so enmeshed that he had to be cut free and even after that, lifting him was no easy task because terror had taken over and was preventing him from co-operating. Pumped with adrenaline his legs jerked and flayed in all directions as he spluttered and gulped in a storm of water.

But at last he was free and in the kitchen being towelled dry; a task that was finished off with a hairdryer which should have signalled an end to the episode. It did not. Beau remained inert, an unseemly tangle of matted white.

Then an eyelid fluttered, but his pulse was weak and for an anxious half hour there was no other visible sign of life. Our pet was in shock and as I knew he must be kept warm, he was rolled in a blanket and laid in front of the fire.

Unlike humans, however, animals recover quickly. They are either ill or well. For that dreadful half hour Beau was ill; and then, suddenly, he was well again – well enough to bite Bunting's tail when he came too near the fire and soon to scuttle off up the garden after a pigeon. But the incident signalled an end to the glory days of a doughty fisher cat, for from then on he was to remain wary of the pond. His fishing days were over. Years of enjoyable (for him) entertainment at an end. It was final, it was "cold turkey" to all that and he never looked back. Even so, he did permit himself an occasional wander around the surrounding rockery after butterflies and the like, in a half-hearted sort of way.

Fishing had been one thing, getting wet another; Beau had never cared for the wet, and now after his misfortune he actively detested it, scurrying indoors at the first hint of rain. Once indoors, however, things took on a different perspective. In the garden a rainy day was to be avoided at all costs, but in the warm and behind glass it could provide entertainment, as through the window he would watch street lamps shining their faces in puddles and cars whishing down the lane, or children sloshing their wellingtons in the gutter or along the curb side; and he did not have to bother about damp paws.

Such was Beau's involvement with windows that Bunting also caught the bug and the two became a duo of enthusiastic puddle watchers! Then they turned their attention indoors and it was not to be long before the turning on of a household tap would produce a flutter of similar enthusiasm. Up would jump a cat beside the bath, a wash basin or the kitchen sink and there they would watch the water as it splashed and gurgled on its way. Neither cat showed any fear. Neither took fright and Beau, on occasion, even poked a paw beneath a running tap.

So here there were two sets of rules operating. Those for outside when water and wetness were bad; when a great fuss would be made if any part of the animal, especially a paw, became contaminated, necessitating a considerable display of "washing" the area dry. For it was not until every particle was pristine and glowing, that the animal could relax. Inside though, things were very different. From another perspective, spectator water sports were not only acceptable but eagerly looked forward to. Viewed through glass, rain and puddles were fun. Indoors and at close quarters, so were turned on taps and gurgling bath water – especially as it whirl-pooled down the plug hole. And the rules remained constant. The fish pond was to remain out of bounds and the prize of a hefty goldfish now came with a price tag too great for a sensible cat to pay.

But outside or in, old loves were soon to be replaced with new ones – with dangers and excitements too numerous to be itemised here. Ones that will no doubt feature later on for a cat's life is never dull as the ups and downs of feline existence demonstrate.

CHAPTER 22

A Little of This and That

Apart from when he fell into the pond, and apart from the unfortunate incidents with Boss Cat and the stray stoat, Beau had seldom been known to show any fear. True, he had been bested by Boss Cat, but in that instance it was wounded pride more than anything else that had caused him to be so unhappy. The Beau that we had come to know and love was brave – some might say foolhardy – as when he defied the motor car to fall asleep in the lane, or crept closer to watch tree felling by chainsaw at the bottom of our garden.

Beau was lovable, by now that should be clear, but he was also stubborn and like all domestic animals, and one is tempted to include the human variety, he disliked anything that might disrupt his daily routine.

For example, it was his habit to lie on our lawn in the late afternoon sunshine and should anything prevent him from doing this he would show his annoyance. Special contempt was reserved for the lawn mower, which at best he viewed as an inconvenience and at worst as an outdoor vacuum cleaner to be confronted and sabotaged. So when the lawn was being mown he would go into action. Impervious to the engine's throbbing power and deaf to its increasingly vociferous approach, in a prime example of feline passive resistance, he would lie down in its way to block its path.

Once picked up and removed, he would quickly catch up and repeat the process until weary of it all, we would shut him indoors where, his face pressed against a window, he would continue to register his disapproval in a series of piercing howls. This was to be a pattern of events enacted over and again until something extraordinary happened to change it.

How it occurred was like this. On one occasion, to avoid being "posted" indoors he jumped up into the mower's grass box en route to the compost heap. It was a random, spur of the moment act, but proved a turning point – a watershed in the history of Beau's battle with our lawn mower. For to his astonishment it became a ride that he greatly enjoyed! He enjoyed it so much that from then on whenever the lawn mower appeared, there he was, quick as a flash, upright among the grass cuttings.

So much for Beau. But what of Bunting at this time? One day he was discovered mesmerised, lying flat in a straight line from nose to tail. He was very still. Only his twitching nose was active. Then he assumed a crouching position – extended a paw which he quickly drew back. He had found a prickly ball, discovered a hedgehog, a creature apparently without head or tail; one wholly unfamiliar and which unlike a bird, a mouse or spider would not run and stubbornly refused to move.

It was no use prodding, patting or poking. Bunting had tried all that and had received nothing but pin pricks for his pains. So our marmalade cat looked around for help which sure enough arrived, or was thought to have arrived, in the shape of Beau. But (alas) he also was to prove unequal to the task.

Beau went through the same routine: a sniff and a pat. Then he took a step or two backwards and attempted a running assault. No response. He had another idea. He approached again and tried to lift the creature with his nose and roll it over. It rocked a little but remained fast, so he tried again with the same lack of success. Meantime Bunting retreated to a bed of marigolds and watched as Beau's pink nose became a pincushion in a scenario that had to be ended.

Then at last both cats were deposited indoors where their curiosity was whetted some more. For from a vantage point on the window sill they were to see the "ball" grow legs and scuttle as fast as they could carry it to a hole in the hedge and away. How extraordinary! But they were soon to forget all about it for a "ball" that grew legs was not to compete for long with an even more amazing creature that was soon to appear. One with fiery breath and blazing eye – the autumn bonfire.

When we lit a bonfire both the cats with window- wide eyes would appear from nowhere to watch this animal as it was fed with strange food, hedge cuttings and leaves; would gaze in awe as it roared up in a tower of flame. Neither showed any fear as they sniffed the pungent air, marvelled as sparks like bright needles rained down all around. Yet their ring-side seats were always chosen with an eye for a quick retreat should it be needed. Meanwhile, like children at a firework display they watched the creature flame, and when at last it spluttered to its end, imploding into a dark and distant deep, they were as mystified as when it first sprang to life, trailing ribbons of glory.

Now that it was over, our two silent and expectant cats still waited for something else to happen and not until every vestige of hope had drained did they retreat indoors. For Bunting and Beau had experienced the thrill of their lives. A thrill to be repeated, year upon year, as a dress rehearsal for what was to come. Bonfire night when many more of these torched and terrifying creatures would stalk the night. When our cats were to be kept indoors and away from all the fun because they might get hurt. Because received opinion told us that all cats at such time must be terrified out of their wits which they mostly were. So did Bunting and Beau make the best of bonfires in their own back garden and for "afters" a curl up on a cushion after a hearty supper.

CHAPTER 23

Hunger Strike

Both cats were on hunger strike. It was clear that they had made a pact: no food was to pass their lips until they got what they wanted – whatever that was! Could it really be that they were sick of the freshly cooked white fish so lovingly prepared each day for their tea? Apparently so, for the same routine was enacted each day with monotonous regularity. I would call them in for their supper. "Fish, fish, come on boys, time for supper." And in they would run – ready, salivating and expectant. The dishes were then put out and up they jumped with alacrity onto the utility work top. They had to eat there because any food put on the floor would be gobbled by the dog.

Then the pantomime began. Each approached his dish, walked round it and headed straightway for the other's bowl further away, and in so doing orchestrated a movement not dissimilar to a figure of eight. That was just the beginning, for it was when each arrived at the second dish that the fun really started. First the food was sniffed and sniffed again as if in disbelief. Then a desultory bite would be attempted – then another which served to verify (for them) the awful truth that their meal was uneatable. Astonishment was feigned as each looked round for an alternative menu, and when nothing else was forthcoming, both with a flick of the tail jumped down, leaving me with the distinct impression that it was all my fault!

At first we decided that it was a passing whim, a brief example of aberrant feline behaviour which we did not understand and would soon pass. So I decided to stand firm. The animals were well fed and healthy and they would eat when they were hungry, wouldn't they? But they would not and did not.

So was their food put down and taken up hours later to be served up again the following day. For days, not a bite passed their lips although, keen as ever, they came in at meal times when they were called. "Don't weaken" I said to myself as the days mounted: but by day five the weight that they had lost was beginning to show – their coats were less glossy, or so I thought, and their eyes less bright. It made no difference. They persisted.

By day six my nerve broke and I joined an anxious throng of would-be customers around shelves of cat food in our local supermarket. All the cat owners congregated there had a story to tell; of how Monty had thrived on Catkins until suddenly Felix was in the frame, to be followed by Whiskers and then God knows what…. How Poppy had thrived on Sheba until for some mysterious reason she would eat nothing but dry food. Another owner had heard tell that one brand was produced from horse meat, so we could not buy that, and so it went on……

Tins were picked up and put down. One had to be careful of food with artificial additives, of dry food which might damage the kidneys. Indecision reigned. All were sympathetic to my plight. None had experienced six days of self imposed starvation and marvelled at the sheer tenacity, the extraordinary pig-headedness of my wayward pets but could offer little advice.

In the end I reluctantly bid my new "friends" goodbye and made for the checkout with a bulging trolley of assorted brands, all with endearing portraits of butter-wouldn't-melt, felines on their containers – all with assurances that their products were made from REAL fish or meat which no self respecting cat could fail to enjoy.

Back at home all this was to be put to the test and quickly. For although the cats were not ill they soon would be if they did not eat and I was determined (confound them) that they should have whatever was necessary to keep them well.

So we tried the goodies in rotation. Felix, Whiskers, Go Cat (the picture of the cat on that tin was especially appealing) Sheba, and whatever else I had been able to lay my hands on: but it was all to no avail. The filled saucers were always eagerly awaited, swiftly approached, sniffed.... and discarded and it was not long before I began to think wildly of intravenous drips and all manner of unspeakable endings, skeletal corpses, that sort of thing. Meanwhile our dog was thriving on discarded cat food and as Bunting and Beau dwindled, so her weight proportionately increased. It is an ill wind, they say and so it was.

Then I had an idea! If our much loved dog could happily eat and thrive upon cat food, then might not the process work in reverse? Might not our cats prefer dog food for a change? So a tin of Pal was opened and a spoonful or two of the meat "splodged" onto a couple of saucers and given to them for their supper. In a matter of seconds, or it seemed like seconds, each saucer was licked clean – filled up again and again and licked clean. Then a couple of satisfied "moggies" settled as they had in the past, to sleep contentedly on the settee.

Feeding dog food to our cats lasted nearly a week and during that period they rapidly put on weight and began to regain their former good looks. Perhaps it was time to start feeding them their usual white fish again? Well, it was.... It turned out that they were ready as never before to tackle their specially prepared fish suppers with avidity. It is hard to believe, but they fell upon it and gobbled like turkeys and as their stomachs distended so did their enthusiasm for the food that they had so recently rejected.

How could this be we wondered? But one thing is sure. On occasion it is as difficult to understand the feline mind as it is to comprehend the workings of its affections. Now at supper time our cats were again affectionate. They purred very loudly; they head butted and pawed and rubbed against ankles; they returned to their lovable, former selves.

Hunger strike! What hunger? It was past, finished and over. It was forgotten, and what is more, it really did happen.

Chloe

As has been mentioned, Beau disliked most other cats on principle, and to this end he worked hard to keep them "off" his territory which included not only our garden, but a good stretch of the quiet road in which we lived as well. That was in theory, but life, even for a cat and especially if that cat were Beau, is sometimes less straight forward. Take for example Chloe, the cat next door. Chloe was a rescued cat like ours and like them she, too, had grown into a magnificent specimen. As a kitten she had been found starving and fending for herself far from adequately, because she was so young. Her eyes were two large black pools, her fur was matted and she was as light to pick up as a baby bird.

That was then, but later it was a very different story, for loving care with excellent food and good grooming had turned her, over the weeks, into a long haired tabby with a silky coat and eyes that sparkled and changed colour with the coming out and going in of the sun. Now not only was Chloe very beautiful, but more to the point she was also a good fisherman. This placed Beau in a bit of a quandary because although the fish she caught, and could be seen to have caught as she paraded with it in her mouth, was not from "his" pool (that would have been out of the question) he resented her prowess and wanted what he could not have. And as for several weeks she would turn up scurrying through our garden with her latest victim in her mouth, it presented him with a problem.

In the first place he did not want her in "his" garden and certainly not near "his" pool, but on the other hand the fish that was dangling so tantalisingly from her jaws reminded him of his own lack of achievement in this field. This was especially true because he was going through a "bad patch", his own endeavours in this field having yielded precious little reward in spite of hours of trying. And he did not take kindly to playing second fiddle or even no fiddle at all as he had frequently come away from our pool with nothing to show for the effort he had expended. So he did not chase her away. He attempted to follow her and find out where she was heading but when she saw him she quickly changed her plans and played the innocent, rolling in our bed of nasturtiums or chasing shadows in the shrubbery. And should he get within pouncing distance, she was off!

Beau was not the only concerned party. Valerie, her owner, was as keen as our pet to find out from where these fish were being taken. So were we, and all of us had as little success in our endeavours as our white cat. On a number of occasions, Valerie did manage to tempt Chloe with food and grab the unfortunate captive, which between us we managed to re-cycle into our terrace pond. But these were quite big fish – quite valuable, and although our friend did not want to broadcast to all the neighbours that her cat was depleting somebody's fish stocks, she did want the thieving to stop and to find out where the "crime" was being committed.

What could be done? Beau had tried his best. He even in a tentative sort of way tried to make friends with Chloe, allowing her free passage across "his" land. Then he hid and tried to follow her but she would have none of it and always seemed to be a step ahead. I made use of Google, homing in on local gardens, searching for fish ponds and feeling like a voyeur. Nothing came up.

Meanwhile the fish kept appearing. Beau decided that he had had enough and started chasing her. It was fruitless. By now we counted that Chloe had "stolen" up to a dozen or so fish, a number of which we had managed to "re-cycle" (our pond was now a thriving cauldron of activity) while others she proudly paraded, taking care that Beau should see but not get too close.

This little saga should have a proper ending. But the truth is that we never did find out from where Chloe was filching her fish. But it does have an ending of sorts, for after a few weeks when our fish pond was bursting with contraband, the thieving suddenly stopped. As abruptly as it started it ceased! Our next door cat returned to her former pursuits and was to be seen without a hint of a fish in her mouth! To this Beau responded by making it clear that she was no longer welcome on our side

Chloe.

of the fence. Without a fish there was to be no admittance – no longer any legitimate access, and to prove his point he puffed himself up and looked fierce. Chloe remained unconcerned, though she did skirt round our garden on her way to more rewarding pleasures.

What had happened can only be surmised. Perhaps the hapless fish owner had at last woken up to the fact that his fish needed better protection. If so, it had taken him several weeks and the loss of much stock before any action was taken. Or perhaps Chloe had simply bled the stock dry – or a fierce dog had at last warned her off.

Or maybe our beautiful, next door cat had found it all too easy and simply become bored with fishing and decided to give it a miss. But whatever the reason it was over. Another chapter was closed as each animal returned to life as it had been before. As Beau in his own garden, once again, reigned supreme – supreme enough to try his hand at fishing again – from his own pool.

CHAPTER 25

Fox Watch

It was late summer and Bunting and Beau were enjoying, not the last of the summer wine, but the last of the sun as it prepared to sink behind the tree tops. They lay on the lawn, Bunting on his back with front paws drawn up to his chin, his back legs and tail stretched out in a straight line. His eyes were shut, but his ears and nose were hard at work. Everything that whizzed, buzzed or zinged; every patrolling ladybird or scurrying beetle was registered and soon to be recycled in his dreams.

Beau lay on his side, his nose and left cheek half buried in the green turf. His front paws were a pair of crossed keys and his back legs trailed luxuriously. Like Bunting his ears and nose were hard at work, but unlike the other cat his eyes (or the one that could be seen) was open, its gaze vacant as an empty saucer of milk.

Their apparent calm, however, was deceptive. For in reality both cats were marking time, getting themselves "hyped up" for what was to come. They were waiting for dusk and its ever deepening veil – for the moon to ripen; and for something else which was to provide a grand finalé to their day.

For all that had previously happened: tea in the garden, the descending saucers of milk, the lazing in the sun had been but a prelude and now a remarkable change was to take place in our pets' demeanour. We had packed up and gone indoors and they had watched the tray being carried and the chairs stacked away with apparent indifference. Still more time....

Then suddenly – from the flick of a tail to the tremble of a whisker they were both awake. Both crouched, excited and agitated – brave and frightened at the same time, their eyes directed with a peculiar intensity towards the creeping shadows in the shrubbery.

By now it was dark and the garden, perfumed with odours of night, provided a perfect setting for what was to come. With military precision the two cats had taken up their positions. These were chosen carefully, on the one hand they must see without being seen and on the other have access to an easy escape route should this be necessary.

Close by the house Beau had mounted and was now straddling the fence, a position which was to afford him a choice and panoramic view. He was crouched long and low, but even so his white coat provided (from my point of view) an eye catching and unwelcome glimmer in the moonlight. Bunting, on the other hand, wedged between the dwarf wall and a couple of flower pots was barely visible, his marmalade coat blending easily into the dark. He had a clear view down the garden and could make a swift getaway into the garden room should he wish. The minutes ticked by … and by. But cats are tuned to wait and watch. They are good at it and get plenty of practice whether it be at a mouse hole, a bird's nest or, as tonight, on fox watch. So they moved not a muscle, each locked into an anticipatory time capsule of their own imaginations.

And tonight the expectations of both cats were to be rewarded! First came the advance warning. They scented the animal when it was several gardens away and their excitement mounted. But still they waited – until suddenly and silently the long awaited fox emerged from the shadows at the top of the garden only to disappear again into the shrubbery before striking out down a footpath towards the house. What a beauty he was! A young male in the prime of life with a magnificent brush of a tail and eyes that glowed when caught in a gleam of moonlight as he drew nearer and nearer.

The cats froze. Beau – a pencil-slim gleam in the gloom, clung on to his fence; Bunting sank lower and lower. The fox came closer until he reached the patio where he loitered a moment beside the pool before lifting his head and uttering a series of shrill barks. Then with consummate ease, he leapt over our six foot fence and was away. It all happened so quickly; before I had time to rush out and "save" our cats; before they had time to find their legs and run for it.

In fact, they had been safe enough. Our fox was clearly following a scent and had ignored the proximity of Beau and Bunting of whom he must have been well aware. But our cats were not to know this. All they knew was that the excitement they had craved had turned sour and they had been very frightened.

So like bullets from a gun, they were inside the house before the back door could be fully opened. Their hearts pounded, their coats bristled, but a lesson had been learned. Fox watching is fine, so long as it takes place from behind glass which is what they were to do in future. Stake a claim, mount a sill – and wait. This way they still got their thrills – but not the spills, so as to speak!

This way they would live to tell the tale.

CHAPTER 26

Trouble, Trouble

Beau was surveying his kingdom from the front garden wall. That was then. The wall was covered in moss and home to many kinds of interesting insects from the stately black beetle with its boot-polished back, to the smallest spider. Beau had an eye for them all and would watch and wait with little ill intent as they scurried up and around and between his paws.

From his vantage point, if he chose, he could also see the wider world. Children on scooters as they raced along the pavement, babies in prams or women with shopping baskets. Should he wish he might watch them round the corner and disappear – his world unwinding and rewinding as he gazed blandly around.

Sometimes he would stay on "his" wall all morning, moving only to arch his neck for a stroke as people passed. Nearly all responded, to be rewarded with a purr and a nuzzle and those who did not were subject to a grim stare of disapproval. However, there were times when he did not feel at all sociable and then he would lie with his tail wrapped around his eyes and his pink nose, shielding his privacy in a most obvious manner, the feline equivalent of "do not disturb".

On this occasion his mood was ebullient. It was a pleasant summer's day and the moss upon which he was lying made him a soft, warm couch. Beau's eyes reflected the serene blue of the sky and in a spirit of relaxed anticipation he was content to watch and wait and when appropriate, to make contact.

That morning, our pet had been keen to race outside; had arrived to take up his position on the wall at around seven o'clock before the lane became busy with school children and shoppers. Later he was seen by many as they set out for work. He was still there at lunch time, was spoken to by the children opposite at three that afternoon on their way home from school. They remembered how he had fluffed up and stretched his neck for a stroke. And then he was gone, the only evidence for him ever having been around was the small indentation in the moss on top of the wall where he had spent the previous happy hours. Nobody was concerned. After all that is what cats do. They are here one minute and gone the next to return, not at our convenience, but theirs.

So the afternoon and the evening wore on; and when there was no sign of him by supper time when he would always arrive on the dot, salivating and ready to eat, we began to feel a little uneasy. Beau's name was called and called. Then we searched the garden with Bunting at our heels, getting under our feet and making a nuisance of himself in his desire to stay close. But at least he was *there*. We knew where he was. By now it was getting dusk and panic had taken over. He must have been lured away by a cat thief! Visions of him bundled into an unmarked van, or tied up in a sack or in any way being harmed, loomed large.

Then the phone rang. It was a neighbour from down the road, an elderly gentleman who lived a few doors away from us and who had heard us calling our pet. He knew Beau well and would always stop for a chat when our cat was around. He had something to report. Late in the afternoon, he had seen Beau being wheeled down the road in a child's doll pram. The animal had looked quite happy, was sitting bolt upright and was not being restrained in any way, so he had not thought it necessary to take any action: but with hindsight.... He was unable to supply any more information except, he racked his brains, that a small fair haired girl was pushing the pram and that her mother, walking beside her, was wearing jeans and smoking. It was not much to go on. But we thanked Mr Evans and set about taking some action.

First the other animals had to be fed and then we set out. For three hours we tramped the streets, knocking on doors and enquiring if anyone knew of a little fair-haired girl with a doll's pram. They did not. Until, that is, we came down an alleyway to a street of terrace houses and noticed outside one of them, next to a bicycle propped up against the front wall, a small doll's pram! Could it be the one? It was too much to hope, but I rang the bell anyway. A young woman with a cigarette in her mouth opened the door.

"Yes" she articulated and it was not clear whether this was a question or an answer. It hardly mattered for then my husband went through the by now familiar routine. Had she seen a white cat? The response was immediate and dramatic. She most certainly had and a young child was dragged forward to prove it. A sleeve was rolled up and a long livid scar from elbow to wrist exposed. We both expressed horror but dared to enquire if she knew where the animal now was? She most certainly did! It was locked in a cupboard in an outhouse at the rear of the house; and when her husband returned, fortunately he was on nights; she would see that the creature was exterminated.

She was determined and we equally so that he should be spared. We had to get Beau out of his prison – but how? After some desultory talk which achieved little: "May I see him?" I asked, and to our surprise she agreed, but only on condition that the "creature" was not allowed to escape. So we followed her through the house and into a small brick scullery where the door was briskly closed prior to the opening of the cupboard. And there he was! Our beautiful Beau, crouched and terrified, his ears back and his tail trailing in a puddle of oil which had leaked from an overturned can. Then the cupboard was closed with a bang and the young woman moved to the outer door. I could bear it no longer and was actually considering physical force when my husband, Geoffrey, saved the day.

Out came his wallet. "We would like" he said, "your daughter to see a private doctor." The red mist before my eyes flickered, ten, twenty, thirty...

fifty pounds were pressed into the woman's hands. "But first" he said, "we must take the animal away to where he can do no more harm." There was now a gleam in the mother's eye. "One hundred pounds" she said, "Maisy was very frightened." So one hundred pounds it was and never was an animal popped so quickly into a cat basket and away as was Beau at that moment.

So he came home. Fearful and terrified he watched limply and with dilated pupils as we bathed him and offered him food. He seemed dazed and dizzy and behind his left ear we found a deep and jagged gash. Our vet came; and after his injury was thoroughly cleaned, Beau was sedated to wake the following day, still fearful but with a hint of normality in his eye. And return to normal he did – but it took some time during which his absence from the wall was noticed by friends and neighbours alike who came to commiserate and enquire after his health.

We never got to the bottom of what had happened but something very unpleasant must have occurred to make him react the way he did. From then on he was to give our front wall a wide berth. Instead he lay in the drive, nearer to the house where he felt safer. And, sadly, he never fully regained his confidence in children which with hindsight, was perhaps not such a bad thing after all.

CHAPTER 27

Holidays

The year turned and soon it would be holidays again – a time to look forward, to anticipate and savour. So was the credit; but also there was debit in the form of our cats; for unlike dogs you cannot take them with you.

All the catteries I have seen bear a striking resemblance to prisons and one can understand why, for it is not possible to have cats romping around outside in a buttercup meadow. They have to be secure and that means that the animals are incarcerated. So it was that the prospect of a holiday would also fill me with images of gloom. Stories of cats going into a decline from the moment that they viewed the travelling basket; or of dogs (for most kennels also necessitated a degree of confinement) having to be dragged to the car ready to transport them – and all in such a state of terror that preparations must take place at the last minute to minimise the stress, meant that our home was not the happy place that it should have been at this time of year. For ages this had been a problem in our household; one which was difficult to resolve.

Beau would be the first to appreciate that there was something up, that change was in the air. He picked up the vibes – the coming and going and the generally increased activity of which he clearly disapproved. He would become ever present, sitting on the ironing board, lying on piles of newly ironed clothes and generally getting in the way in an obvious attempt to thwart our plans. Soon Bunting would join in, looking abject and only the dog remained unperturbed and placid until she saw the suitcases which up until then we had kept hidden. Then she, too, joined the I-want-to-be-with-you lobby and a general air of misery prevailed.

That was how things used to be, until we met Eileen who ran, not so much a business as a holiday home for cats and dogs. I am sure that she made very little money for herself but she raised a good deal for animal charities and was doing a job she loved. We had met, as is often the case, by accident when out walking the dog. She was remonstrating, very forcibly, with a couple of lads with shot guns who were shooting squirrels and I went to her aid. It would be nice to be able to say that we "converted" them, but at least we managed to encourage them to move away and who knows, it could be that, come time, they did change their minds. It is certainly true that I never saw them again.

That was how we got talking and how I learned of the excellent work she was doing; how we first came to take our own pets to her. After that, when we told Button that she was going on her holidays and showed her the cat basket (for they all went off together) she would wag her tail and bark her delight. Then it would be the cats' turn to wave and weave their tails in a balletic display of joint approval.

Then the cat basket was viewed, not as a prison, but a means to an enjoyable end. A gateway to a new experience. It was nudged and sniffed and walked round: on occasion even entered into as if to make sure that it was still the right size. All such manifestations we viewed with relief, even if tinged with a fleeting moment of regret that life without us was now to be viewed as such an attraction!

So it was that every year the animals were taken to Eileen who greeted them like her own children. First Button would be led away with her tail high, although she would honour us with a fleeting, backward glance as she disappeared; then it was the cats' turn as they were let out of their basket into airy and capacious cages.

I remember going to fetch them all last year. It was our first task upon arriving home and certainly the most enjoyable. We joined a queue of cars with owners all waiting to collect their pets. To kill time, I got out and walked round to be greeted with a sound that was music to my ears. A deep sonorous bark, verified by a fleeting glance on tiptoe over the fence as belonging to Button as she snapped her heels and raced around the meadow with a brown labrador. It must have been "break time" and she was enjoying every moment. But of course there was no sign of the cats. To see them we must first move up the queue to the office and pay our bill. They would be indoors in the airy and white-washed stable block where we would soon be heading.

Formalities over, we were on our way at last to the block where the cats' cages were. These were large and two tiered; the upper for sleeping and the lower, complete with a run, for living, and faced each other across a wide, central gangway. The building was large and entered via a series of double doors which exited from a small lobby. "This is where we have to be careful" said Eileen, "we don't want Beau to run out!" How could he run out? I thought, when he was secure in his cage. But he was not! He was patrolling the walkway with Jennifer who was in the middle of some Saturday morning house cleaning. Eileen looked apologetic as she explained that he was quite safe. That he was allowed out because he did so enjoy fraternising with the other cats! Beau enjoying the company of other cats, when at home he made a point of hating them all on sight? Clearly things here were different. Indeed they were. For here he was dancing from one cage to another with his magnificent tail aloft and his fur fluffed to emulate a cuddly toy. And then he saw us! Flew, scattering Jennifer's mop and brush along the way as he headed in our direction and jumped up nuzzling his head in my arms....

Then it was into the cat basket and home, but not before we had collected Bunting – not before Eileen had explained that cats, as a rule, were never out of their cages unless they were being cleaned. But Beau was different. One day he had hopped out – and somehow it had become a habit, Beau and Jennifer doing the rounds together! Again she assured us that he had always been safe and we knew that he was. That he was, as she said, "not like other cats". Indeed, he was not like any other animal, cat or dog, that we had ever owned. He was simply himself.

Having secured our white cat, it was then Bunting's turn. We approached his cage to find that he was not at home: and then we saw him pressed up against the far wall of his sleeping quarters. He watched as the cage was opened but did not move and made no sound.

Resisting all efforts to pluck him out, he clung on miserably and stubbornly in what was almost a re-run of his time up that fir (wobbly) tree in our garden. At last like a mussel prized from its shell, we got him out and into the cat basket beside Beau, but not before he had retreated a second time and still managed to look as if all hope was lost.

We were disappointed and nonplussed. Eileen assured us that during his stay he had been perfectly happy patrolling his cage and purring when his food arrived. That he had settled in as well as always. Then an explanation presented itself. Beau's cage had been opposite his so that the two cats could see each other. Now it was empty and Beau was safe in his basket. He was nowhere to be seen and possibly our red cat had felt deserted.

As things turned out, this might have been the explanation, for as soon as they were together in the car our red cat became himself – his roly-poly, placid self. He relaxed and his taut muscles eased. He responded to Button's exuberant presence with a rumbling purr and back at home a large dinner restored him in a jiffy to as good as new. Soon all animals were in their favourite places on the hearthrug or a chosen knee: and when Eileen rang up to be reassured, we were able to report, quite definitely, that all was well.

CHAPTER 28

Collars for Christmas

Both our cats were chipped, that was only sensible. But a friend suggested that putting them in collars might be an added precaution against problems that could occur much nearer to home – like getting locked in a neighbour's shed, for example, or in his house. I was doubtful. In the first place, everybody in the area knew Beau anyway and as for Bunting? He so seldom strayed that buying a collar for him seemed, to put it mildly, superfluous. So the idea was shelved for the time being at least.

But I had not counted on our friend's persistence. Had we bought our pets collars yet? We had not, and it was then that she revealed her plan "B". Why not allow her to buy the cats their collars – for Christmas? We wriggled a little uncomfortably, but the idea of collars as Christmas presents was difficult to refuse without seeming ungracious. So collars it was going to be.

The day at last approached and with it two neat little packages from our local pet shop. I knew what they contained and was far from eager to open them but as Angela, our friend, would be coming to see us shortly and would expect to see our animals "kitted" in their new finery, I took a breath and undid the wrapping.

What emerged was kindly meant. Both collars were in part elastic, a necessary precaution as no-one would want our pets to end up dead, swinging from a branch in our garden. Especially as they had each survived such perilous beginnings – Beau having been rescued from near starvation, and Bunting from drowning.

That however was the only resemblance. For from then on Angela had allowed her creative flair for which in other circumstances she could be justly proud, to rather run away with her.

First to be unwrapped was Bunting's collar. It had been carefully chosen (designed) might be a better word to match his marmalade fur and was constructed out of what looked like a series of interlocking and crenellated tassels. They were pink and shiny and boasted a "golden" clasp which clipped with an authoritative clunk. Dangling from one of the tassels was a heart shaped name tag, also in gold, and on which was engraved his name and address in a flowing script. The effect was startling, an adornment better suited to an oriental lady reclining upon a couch than to a marmalade moggie from suburbia.

Beau's collar was unwrapped next. It was made of a stiff, silver brocade, delicately crafted with a "silver" front buckle from which also dangled his name tag, engraved with a border of what looked suspiciously like a series of corn dollies! Silver no doubt to match his coat but certainly not his personality. Brocade more suited to a lady's ball gown than a rough and tumble cat's collar. We could not bring ourselves to use them and they were put away until nearer the time of Angela's visit when she would expect to see them on display. So well meant, such a catastrophe!

Unfortunately, the deadline rapidly approached as deadlines do, when we felt that it was time (literally) for a dress rehearsal. Beau's collar went on first and then Bunting's and it has to be said that they both looked pretty silly. Beau's long haired coat became entangled in the fabric and instead of flowing freely, ruckled like corrugated cardboard paper. Bunting's neck seemed to bulge above and below the contraption (because that is what it was) and he came to resemble a kind of prehistoric monster – one with a small head and enormous body. Not only did they look silly but they were both uncomfortable. They scratched, they bit and they itched. They drove themselves mad and then they rushed off into the sunset and disappeared. We did not know whether to be relieved or worried.

In fact we did not have time to worry for long which was a good thing, for when they came back, which they did in a couple of hours or so, the collars were gone! Hallelujah I thought, and then remembered Angela. Well it couldn't be helped. She would have to be thanked and then told the truth.

Then it occurred to us that perhaps we should make some effort to retrieve the wretched collars! After all they had been a present and the gesture was well meant. So rather half-heartedly we walked up and around the garden and, as expected, came up with nothing. Well, at least the cats were now looking more like themselves, showed no resentment and had clearly put the unfortunate episode behind them. So did we, but the story is not quite finished yet. For having had our supper and fed the animals and settled for a quiet evening, the door bell rang. On the front step was our friend and

Much tastier from a jug.

neighbour, wearing an incredulous expression and holding in his hand Bunting's collar! "I have found this" he said, wiggling it, "dangling from one of the branches of our plum tree!"

Bunting up a tree? I was incredulous, David was incredulous, we were all incredulous! Bunting who after his night long experience up our fir tree had never dared to leave terra firma, who never ventured much further than "his" flower pots.... What on earth had he been doing up a plum tree in next door's garden?

David was invited in and told the saga of the collars. No one had seen Bunting, but he must have been there. He must have climbed that tree, which just shows that when pushed, animals will do extraordinary things.

It would tie up the parcel neatly to be able to say that Beau's collar was also found. Well it was but not for some time, when a few weeks on it turned up at the bottom of a compost heap. "I don't think its wearable now," said Mr Anderson, another of Beau's admirers. "But I thought you might like to have it back."

With a smile I took the miserable strip of blackened brocade and thanked him. Now this did make some sense. Removing and burying the hated thing – that was my Beau running true to form. And as for Angela? We thanked her and explained what had happened, and she took it like the true friend that she was. A fraction disappointed, but prepared to accept the inevitable.

CHAPTER 29

All Good Things...

So the weeks and months passed without us noticing. By now I kept telling people that Beau was seven years old and Bunting six. One day Geoffrey asked me if I knew that this was untrue. But why should I lie? I was indignant because it was what I really believed. But it was not true. By now Beau had arrived at the grand old age of twelve and Bunting was a fraction younger. Possibly, because cats do not age as dogs do - they do not go grey, for example, the ageing process is not so apparent. Or possibly, I just wanted to believe that they were younger, wanted things to carry on and on. Once pointed out, however, it was a shock to realise how effortlessly the years had slipped by.

Both cats looked fit and were as agile as ever. But upon reflection, their horizons had been gradually contracting. Beau no longer went hunting a mile away in the local woods. Instead his nocturnal adventures consisted in crouching under the bonnet of our car parked for his convenience in the drive. At six o'clock he took up his position and at eight o'clock came trotting in for his supper.

Under the car he felt safe, could see without being seen. From there he watched the bobbing headlights of cars as they rounded the corner and caught in their beams, his eyes glowed like little lamps. So he tracked the oncoming and disappearing traffic, creatures with eyes like full moons that pierced the very soul of darkness and sent shivers of excitement along his spine. It was entertainment of which he never tired, moving his head as he waited for the next arrival to appear. Then it was time to stop the "game" or whatever it was, and race indoors, for his timekeeping was such as would have pleased the strictest of employers!

As for Bunting? Never adventurous at the best of times, now he became even less so, only leaving the security of his flower pots for the security of the fireside. Evangeline was a distant dream and, as always, he never forgot to about turn and face the door – ready, should it be necessary for a quick exit before settling himself comfortably on a knee.

Indoors they took up new hobbies. Beau had always been partial to the piano and now when it was played, would curl up beside the pedals where the sound must have been deafening. It was a strange place to drift off to sleep where, after a short spell, he often did! Then Bunting, his shadow, would soon follow, would peep round the door to check that all was well before jumping up on top of the instrument, to be deafened too.

One evening the sound of a car back firing woke them both up and Beau in a fright jumped up on to the piano keys. Strangely, the resultant cacophony, far from terrifying him encouraged him to race up and down the keyboard like a child paddling in water. This was fun and from then on, when one of us wanted to play, he would always leap up and attempt to join in. Meanwhile Bunting re-discovered the delight of cotton reels which he propelled forward with a gentle pat, his aim to watch the twine unwind, to bite it and shake it as it unravelled.

So did our two cats continue to flourish; on summer afternoons, paddling in pools of sunlight and on wet winter days, cosy indoors, snuggled by the fire. They remained our delight and never a thought was given to how things might end as we watched them pursue their various ways, crisscrossing their secret feline world with the cosy human one.

Beau grew more knowing than ever. He had always been able to open kitchen cupboards and now he turned his attention to the fridge for he knew that inside was food. He never succeeded in opening it but not for the want of trying. Balanced on his back legs he tried using both front paws to insert his claws in the gap at the side of its door. This meant that he had to lean like a tree in the wind, a little to one side with his right paw above his left, while at the same time balancing his body against the white enamel of the freezer below. Of course he had neither the strength nor the body weight to achieve his object, but undeterred, again and again he continued to attempt the impossible. And even if he had been able to open the door, he would not have reached the food as the shelves were too full and too high. But, doomed to failure as he was, one could not but admire our cat's determined assaults which lasted for weeks rather than days.

It was the telephone that finally provided an alternative distraction. One day when it rang he rushed to the nearest extension and remained there, crouched on guard, until it was answered. He was fascinated by the voice on the other end, listening and looking to see where it came from. Soon this became routine; ring, run and respond by searching for the voice on the other end of the line – an attempt as little likely to be gratified as the opening of the fridge door.

He and Bunting remained as companionable as ever; would settle down, back to back, like a couple of book ends to digest their evening meal. Bunting's eyes were shiny as conkers and he would "smile", in fact both cats "smiled", by slitting their eyes in response to a stroke or a chin tickle.

Both cats remained lithe and supple as, unheeded, the years mounted; until there came a time when Beau arrived at the grand old age of eighteen with Bunting close behind at one year younger. Now they were two of the oldest cats in the borough to visit our vet's surgery for check ups and yearly injections, and the latter was rather proud of them as we were – always delighted when there was a student on the premises to whom he could show them off.

But nothing in this world is permanent and there had to come a time when clouds gathered and obscured the blue. It was Beau who first showed signs of illness. He developed cystitis and then a kidney infection. In the past he had always responded quickly to treatment – but not this time. For this was to be the onset of acute kidney failure and before we knew it we were in the centre of an emotional storm.

Our vet told us that there was little to be done. At this stage antibiotics would be of little help and the problem was set to deteriorate. He gently told us the kindest thing would be to put our beloved Beau to sleep...

But we could not do it. I was selfish and thought only of myself. Of keeping him alive as long as was possible.

In the meantime Beau, a very clean animal dragged himself from drinking bowl to toilet tray in an endless succession of attempts to deal with his excessive thirst and desire to urinate. As the days passed he became exhausted but would not give up – the tray must be reached. Again our vet came to the house. Beau registered his approach with the faintest flick of his tail – but that was all. Then he remained motionless, slumped in his basket with eyes closed. By now our beloved pet had been ill for nearly two weeks. He was going to leave us, that was clear. To put him to sleep was *right*, but the idea of it made us feel dreadful. Even Mr Robson had a brightness in his eye as the lethal injection was delivered into Beau's left front paw.

It was over. The animal relaxed, he had been relieved of his burden and the years rolled away. He was young again – all signs of his suffering gone and as the tears flowed I knew that the right decision had been made. We all inclined our heads and spent a moment in silence. After all, it was the end of a way of life, for us as well as for him. For eighteen years he had been part of our household, punching above his weight, well above it and now he had come to the end of his journey.

Gently and after a final caress, he was carried to Mr Robson's car and placed on a blanket on the back seat. For Beau was to be cremated and his ashes returned and scattered in our garden beneath "his" apple tree. So we said our goodbyes and returned to the house, to Bunting and Button who knew but did not understand what had happened.

That was how it was. We missed Beau every day, but we still had Bunting and, thankful for that, could not have envisaged that one disaster would so swiftly be followed by another. But it was. For our red cat, as we affectionately called him, was to set about searching for Beau as determinedly as all those years ago he had looked for Evangeline. At first when there was no Beau at supper time he was nonplussed, but finally persuaded to eat a mouthful or two before embarking upon his great task which was to search every corner in every room; and outside, every favourite place: the roses, the fish pond, the garden shed; as over and over – day in and out, the hunt continued. He barely ate or slept and all the time he cried, a long drawn out wail of a cry, searching, searching.

We thought that eventually he would settle but we were wrong. For his whole life had been lived under the comforting umbrella of Beau's protection and he could neither understand why nor accept the fact that this was now forever gone. Like a child in deep water who cannot swim, he was floundering.

Soon there was worse to come. It was not to be long before Bunting developed a large obstruction in his colon which grew rapidly. He was taken to see our vet who confirmed the worst and advised with considerable regret that he should also be put to sleep. Again we hesitated, for the thought of losing our second beloved pet so soon after the first was almost too much to contemplate. He was brought home. By now he was heavily sedated, which meant that he was unable to continue his "search". Now he spent his time mostly sleeping on his favourite chair, a shadow of his former tubby self. It could not continue; the quality of his life was so limited.

Like Beau, Bunting was put to rest at home on his favourite chair. Even through the fog of sedation he was able to recognise his friend, our vet, when he arrived and managed to raise his head a little before falling back. Passively he allowed Mr Robson to stroke him and even moved a front paw forward as it was gently held and the final injection administered. So Bunting fell asleep and out of his two-fold misery; the psychological pain of missing an absent friend and the physical pain from the progress of his tumour. It all happened almost four weeks to the day of Beau's loss and as I stroked our marmalade cat for the last time before he, too was taken away, the grief was indescribable.

Fancy all that fuss over a couple of cats people may think. Let them think it! They have never experienced what we are so grateful for, that extraordinary bonding between feline and human which enriched our lives.

So it was that over such a brief spell we were bereft of two of our pets who had given so much joy and whose combined ages totalled nearly thirty-six years. Bunting, too, was to be returned to us and his ashes also scattered in the garden around his beloved flower pots. So in a way they are still with us which is how it should be.

It was the little things we missed. The jumping on laps; the evening's greeting as one cat emerged from under the car and the other from behind those pansy filled pots. The dramas. The chasing of Beau down the road with a goldfish sprouting from his mouth like a giant moustache. Bunting clinging to the branch of an apple tree and not daring to move. So many memories as on a cine film in the mind.

But most of all we missed them for not being there. The empty living room, cold knees and the settee, a silent witness to the fact that they were never going to return. A fact very difficult to come to terms with – for it was like losing two members of a family; on second thoughts it was losing two members, two members of our family.

But at last we managed it and learned to be grateful for the happy times and the delights we shared. Bunting and Beau may no longer be with us in the flesh, but we remember them in our hearts and always will.

CHAPTER 30

Postscript

We were not going to have any more cats; the final heartbreak was not worth it. So for many weeks we put up with the emptiness. We had our well loved dog after all and she was a great comfort.

Then we received a phone call. It was from our vet who felt that, by now, our grieving time was due to expire. Two mackerel tabby kittens had been found dumped in a cardboard box inside a dustbin and a good home was urgently required... I said no, and then upon being persuaded to see them, said yes as he knew I would! That was how we came to open our home to Perdita and Echo – the first who grew up to be placid and tubby, like Bunting and the second with her sense of purpose, her strong likes and dislikes, more like Beau.

Of course they do not replace but complement what we have lost. Different cats are – different, but in them our memories of what used to be are stirred and when I call them in at night, I sometimes get the impression that out there with them are two shadows – one light and one darker, ready to slip inside as well.

It is a very distinct impression. One that provides continuity with the past and revives happy memories. One that ensures that our recollections of Beau and Bunting remain evergreen, even as the future beckons....

Acknowledgements

I would like to thank my friends, Valerie and David Shepherd for offering a photograph of their cat, Chloe; also Pam Hayes for typing the script and offering advice. Finally my thanks must go to my husband, Geoffrey, for the excellent photographs of our pets that he has provided and for his constant support.

Oh so fruity!

BY THE SAME AUTHOR

Rhyme on the Spray (Poetry)	£5.95
A Lady of Letters (Catherine Hutton)	£13.95
The World of William Shenstone (William Shenstone)	£13.95
Chequered Chances (Lady Luxborough)	£12.95
A Sense of Occasion (Mendelssohn)	£10.95

Fore more details please visit: www.brewinbooks.com